500 Sern for Busy Pastors

For more sermon outlines and other great ministry resources, please visit us at:
www.PastorsHelper.com

By Barry L. Davis

Author, Editor, and Compiler

Copyright©2022 Barry L. Davis

ISBN: 9798840549735

GodSpeed Publishing

Note: Outlines come from a variety of sources and have been updated and reformatted.

PERMISSIONS: *If you are the purchaser of this volume you are given the right to use the following sermon outlines to preach/teach. You may use them "as is," or edit them to suit your purposes.* <u>You may not reproduce these outlines to give them away or offer them for sale</u>. *They are for the purchasers use only.*

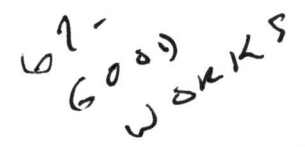

[handwritten: 61 - Good Works]

Introduction

Dear Fellow Preacher,

For most of us, one of the most rewarding, yet difficult tasks, is preparing messages to preach and teach. We are honored by God to stand before our congregation each week, and we want to give them the very best, but with the press of the many demands of ministry, sometimes that is difficult to do.

And if you're like me, you prefer writing your own sermons because you have a special connection with your congregation that is hard to reach through a message someone else has written. In other words, no one knows your people like you do!

This collection of sermon outlines gives you a starting point – a sermon title, and a thoroughly biblical deductive sermon outline. But you are free to "fill-in-the-blanks" so to speak and add your own meat and potatoes to the mix! We invite you to make these messages your own, because only you know the people God has called you to preach to.

May God Bless You as You Share His Word!

In Christ,

Barry L. Davis, D.Min., Ph.D.

Table of Contents

Introduction 3

1. AARON AND HIS SONS 23
2. A.B.C. OF ACTS 2 23
3. A.B.C. OF THE GOSPEL 23
4. ABOUNDING 23
5. ABRAHAM'S SERVANT 24
6. ACCEPTABILITY 24
7. ACCEPTABLE SACRIFICES 24
8. AFAR OFF 24
9. "ALL" 25
10. THE ALL'S OF COLOSSIANS 25
11. ALONE 25
12. ALWAYS 26
13. THE AMALEKITE 26
14. ANDREW AND HIS BROTHER 26
15. APOLLOS 27
16. ARISE 27
17. "AS HE IS SO ARE WE" 27
18. ASPECTS OF CHRIST 28
19. ATTITUDE OF THE BELIEVER 28
20. BARTIMEUS 28
21. BE HOLY 29
22. THE BELIEVER 29
23. BELIEVERS BELONG TO CHRIST 29
24. THE BELIEVER'S BENEFITS 29
25. THE BELIEVER'S CALLING 30
26. THE BELIEVER'S PATHWAY 30

27. THE BELIEVER'S POSITION 31

28. THE BELIEVER'S PRIVILEGES 31

29. BELIEVING 31

30. THE BELOVED 32

31. THE BETTER PROMISES 32

32. BETTER THINGS 32

33. BEYOND DESCRIPTION 33

34. BLESSINGS OF THE BELIEVER 33

35. BLESSINGS PROMISED 33

36. THE BODY 33

37. THE BOOK 34

38. BROUGHT 34

39. THE CARE OF THE SHEPHERD FOR THE SHEEP 34

40. THE CAVE OF ADULLAM 35

41. CERTAINTIES 35

42. CHARACTERISTICS OF TRIBE OF GAD 36

43. THE CHILD OF GOD 36

44. THE CHILD OF GOD SHOULD BE ABLE — 36

45. THE CHILD OF GOD SHOULD BE STEDFAST 36

46. CHRIST'S EXPECTATIONS FOR US 37

47. CHRIST IS ALL AND IN ALL 37

48. THE CHURCH SPOKEN OF 37

49. THE COMING OF THE LORD TEACHES 38

50. THE COMMON SALVATION 38

51. COMPLETE DELIVERANCE 38

52. A CONDESCENDING GOD 39

53. CONDITION OF THE CHURCHES 39

54. CONDITIONS TO EFFECTUAL PRAYER 39

55. CONQUERING POWER	39
56. THE CONSCIENCE	40
57. CONSIDER	40
58. CONTINUING	40
59. CONVERSATION	40
60. 1 CORINTHIANS 6	41
61. 2 CORINTHIANS 5	41
62. 2 CORINTHIANS 6:17-18	41
63. COUPLETS IN MATTHEW 7	42
64. DAILY LIVING FOR THE CHRISTIAN	42
65. DAVID'S THREE ATTITUDES	42
66. DAVID'S WORKMEN	42
67. DEAD WITH CHRIST	43
68. DEUTERONOMY 31:12	43
69. THE DEVELOPMENT OF FAITH	43
70. THE DEVELOPMENT OF GRACE	44
71. THE DEVELOPMENT OF WORKS	44
72. DOUBLE TITLES GIVEN TO THE LORD JESUS	44
73. EIGHT CHARACTERISTICS OF THE WICKED	44
74. EIGHT CONDITIONS OF HAPPINESS	45
75. EIGHT CONTRASTS IN PSALM 107	45
76. EIGHT THINGS ABOUT JONAH	46
77. EIGHT THINGS GOD DOES IN PSALM 107	46
78. EIGHT THINGS GOD WAS TO DAVID	47
79. EIGHT THINGS IN ABUNDANCE	47
80. EIGHT THINGS TO FIND	47
81. EIGHTFOLD DELIVERANCE	48
82. ENDURES FOR EVER	48

83. ENOCH 48

84. EPHESIANS 1 49

85. EPHESIANS 2 49

86. EPHESIANS 2:13 49

87. EPHESIANS 5:8 49

88. EPISTLE TO PHILEMON 50

89. ETERNAL THINGS IN JUDE 50

90. THE EUNUCH 50

91. EZRA 6 50

92. FAILURE OF THE DISCIPLES 51

93. FAITH 51

94. FAITH'S FUNDAMENTALS 52

95. FAITH'S TRIUMPHS 52

96. FELIX 52

97. FELLOWSHIP 53

98. FIRE 53

99. FIVE ASPECTS OF CRUCIFIXION 53

100. FIVE ASPECTS OF FRUIT-BEARING IN PAUL'S LIFE 53

101. FIVE CLASSES 54

102. FIVE CLASSES AT THE CROSS 54

103. FIVE EXHORTATIONS IN COLOSSIANS 54

104. FIVE WAYS OF DOING THE LORD'S WORK 54

105. FIVEFOLD RESULT OF HIS WORK 55

106. THE FLESH 55

107. FOR HIS NAME'S SAKE 55

108. FORGIVENESS 56

109. FOUR APPEARINGS 56

110. FOUR ASPECTS OF THE FEAST 56

111. FOUR ASPECTS OF THE LORD JESUS	56
112. FOUR BLESSED STATEMENTS CONCERNING JESUS	57
113. FOUR PLACES FOR FOUR KINDS OF CHRISTIANS	57
114. FOUR CRIES FOR MERCY	57
115. FOUR DECEITFUL THINGS	57
116. FOUR GREAT THINGS	57
117. FOUR HANDWRITINGS	58
118. FOUR LIVELY THINGS	58
119. FOUR MANIFESTATIONS OF THE LORD	58
120. FOUR MEN IN LUKE 5	58
121. FOUR P's IN PSALM 42	59
122. FOUR POURINGS OUT	59
123. FOUR QUESTIONS PUT TO JONAH	59
124. FOUR "REMEMBERS"	59
125. FOUR SNARES TO WATCH AGAINST	59
126. FOUR STEPS	60
127. THE FOUR SUPPERS	60
128. FOUR THINGS ABOUT JONAH	60
129. FOUR THINGS GOD DOES FOR ME	60
130. FOUR THINGS GOD PREPARED FOR JONAH	60
131. FOUR THINGS MEN LOVE	61
132. FOUR THINGS SAID OF THE UNSAVED	61
133. FOUR THOUGHTS ABOUT ISRAEL	61
134. FOURFOLD ASPECT OF THE WORD	61
135. FOURFOLD DESCRIPTION OF OURSELVES	62
136. FOURFOLD VIEW OF GOD	62
137. FOURFOLD WITNESSING	62
138. FRUIT BEARING	62

139. GENESIS 1 63

140. GIDEON 63

141. GIFTS FROM THE LORD 63

142. GLORY 64

143. GOD 64

144. GOD'S CAUTIONS 64

145. GOD'S FAITHFULNESS TO ISRAEL 65

146. GOD'S GRACE SHOWN TO ISRAEL 65

147. GOD'S "I WILL" 66

148. GOD'S INTEREST IN HIS PEOPLE 66

149. GOD'S PURPOSE IN CHASTENING 66

150. GOD'S THREE APPOINTMENTS 66

151. GOD'S THREE FINDINGS 66

152. GOOD WORKS 67

153. THE GOSPEL IN JOB 33 67

154. GRACE 67

155. THE GRIEVOUS ESTATE OF THE WICKED 68

156. THE GROWTH OF THE BELIEVER 68

157. HE IS ABLE 69

158. HE KNOWS 69

159. HEAVENLY PLACES 69

160. THE HEBREW CAPTIVES 70

161. HELP 70

162. "HIS" 71

163. HIS GLORY 71

164. HIS KINGDOM 71

165. HIS PRESENCE 71

166. HIS VOICE 72

167. HIS WINGS	72
168. HOLY BOLDNESS	72
169. THE HOLY SPIRIT IN EPHESIANS	72
170. THE HOPE	73
171. THE HOPE IN COLOSSIANS	73
172. HOSEA 14	73
173. HOW BOAZ DEALT WITH RUTH	74
174. HOW LONG?	74
175. IMPORTANT QUESTION AND ANSWER	74
176. IN A MOMENT	74
177. IN JEREMIAH WE HAVE	75
178. "IN LOVE"	75
179. IN PHILIPPIANS 4, WE HAVE	75
180. "IN THE LORD"	76
181. THE INHERITANCE	76
182. ISAIAH IN THE TEMPLE	76
183. ISAIAH 55:1-2	77
184. ISAIAH 57:19-20	77
185. ISRAEL BROUGHT OUT OF CAPTIVITY	77
186. ISRAEL IN THE WILDERNESS	77
187. JEHOIAKIM	78
188. JEREMIAH A SERVANT	78
189. JESUS	78
190. JOB 36:18	79
191. JOHN 11:28-29	79
192. JOHN 14	79
193. JOHN'S FOUR-FOLD ATTITUDE	79
194. JOINED UNTO THE LORD	80

195. JONAH ON THE DOWN GRADE	80
196. JONAH'S MESSAGE	80
197. JOSEPH AND HIS BRETHREN	80
198. JOSEPH AND JESUS	81
199. JOTTINGS FROM PSALM 145	82
200. JOY	83
201. THE JUDGMENT	83
202. JUSTIFICATION DEFINED	83
203. JUSTIFICATION, OUR NEED FOR IT	83
204. JUSTIFICATION, OUR SOURCE	84
205. THE KING	84
206. THE LAMB	84
207. LAZARUS	85
208. LESSONS FROM LOT'S WIFE	85
209. LESSONS FROM LUKE 5	85
210. LESSONS FROM RUTH 3	86
211. LESSONS FROM THE AXE HEAD	86
212. LESSONS FROM THE PLAGUE OF HAIL	86
213. LITTLE THINGS WITH GREAT RESULTS	86
214. THE LIVING BREAD	87
215. LOOKING	87
216. THE LORD IS READY	87
217. THE LORD JESUS AND HIS PEOPLE	87
218. THE LORD JESUS IN MARK 1	88
219. THE LORD JESUS IN PSALM 16	88
220. THE LORD'S RETURN	89
221. LOVE	89
222. LOVE'S ADVANTAGES	89

223. LOVED ONES IN GOSPEL OF JOHN 90
224. LOVE'S SACRIFICE 90
225. LUKE 23:33 90
226. MADE 91
227. MAN 92
228. THE MAN IN EPHESIANS 92
229. MANASSEH 92
230. MARKS OF A TRUE SERVANT 93
231. MERCY 93
232. THE MEEK 93
233. MORE EXCELLENT 94
234. THE MORNING 94
235. "MY" IN JOHN'S GOSPEL 94
236. NEHEMIAH HAD SIX FORMS OF OPPOSITION IN HIS WORK 95
237. NEVER 95
238. NICODEMUS 95
239. NINE STEPS IN PETER'S LIFE 95
240. "NO MORE" 96
241. ONE ANOTHER 96
242. OPERATIONS OF THE HOLY SPIRIT 96
243. OUR CROWNING BLESSING 97
244. OUR FEET 97
245. OUR GOD 98
246. OUR GREAT DELIVERER (2 COR 1:10) 98
247. OUR HEARTS 99
248. OUR HOPE 99
249. OUR LIPS 100
250. OUR MOUTHS 100

251. OUR PRIVILEGES AS GOD'S PEOPLE	101
252. OUR RESURRECTION BODY	102
253. OUR UNION WITH CHRIST	102
254. PARTAKERS	102
255. THE PATH	103
256. THE PATIENT AND PHYSICIAN	103
257. PAUL SUFFERED WHAT SAUL INFLICTED	103
258. PAUL'S ACTION IN ACTS 27	104
259. PAUL'S COURSE	104
260. PAUL'S DESIRE	105
261. PAUL'S FAITHFULNESS TO TIMOTHY	105
262. PAUL'S THREEFOLD THANKSGIVING	105
263. PAUL'S TWOFOLD EXPERIENCE	105
264. PEACE	105
265. PEACE AND NO PEACE	106
266. PEACE IN TWO ASPECTS	106
267. PERFECTION	106
268. PERFECTION OF THE LORD JESUS	107
269. PICTURE OF A RIGHTEOUS MAN	107
270. PICTURE OF MAN IN THE BOOK OF JOB	107
271. PILGRIM'S PROGRESS IN PSALM 63	108
272. THE PLACE	108
273. POWER OF THE TRINITY	108
274. POWER PRINCIPLES	108
275. PRAYER	109
276. PRAYER (2)	109
277. PRECIOUS THINGS	111
278. THE PRE-EMINENT ONE	111

279. PRIVILEGES AND RESPONSIBILITIES 111
280. PROOFS OF CHRIST'S LOVE TO THE CHURCH 112
281. PSALM 4 112
282. PSALM 16:11 113
283. PSALM 23 (version 1) 113
284. PSALM 23 (version 2) 113
285. PSALM 23 (version 3) 114
286. PSALM 32 114
287. PSALM 40 114
288. PSALM 59:16 115
289. PSALM 63 115
290. PSALM 84 115
291. PSALM 86 115
292. PSALM 136 116
293. THE PSALMIST'S DETERMINATION 116
294. THE PURSUIT OF JOY 116
295. QUANTITIES OF FRUIT 117
296. QUALITY OF FRUIT 117
297. THE QUEEN OF SHEBA 117
298. RAHAB 117
299. READY 118
300. REALITIES 118
301. REASONS FOR NOT FEARING 118
302. RECONCILIATION IN 2 Cor. 5:18-20 119
303. REDEMPTION 119
304. REJOICING 120
305. REPENTANCE 120
306. REPRESENTATIVE PERSONS IN PSALM 23 121

307. RESULT OF A PRAYER MEETING 121

308. RESULT OF PETER'S PREACHING ON THE DAY OF PENTECOST 121

309. RESULTS OF OVERCOMING 122

310. REVELATION 21:6 122

311. THE REWARD.. 122

312. THE RICH FARMER 123

313. THE ROCK 123

314. THE ROCK OF 123

315. ROMANS 3:23-25 124

316. ROMANS 3:27-29 124

317. RUTH 124

318. RUTH'S SERVICE 124

319. THE SAINTS ARE TO BE 125

320. THE SAINT'S POSITION 125

321. SALVATION 125

322. SALVATION DESCRIBED 126

323. SALVATION IS 126

324. SAMUEL... 126

325. SAUL'S CONVERSION.. 126

326. THE SAVIOR 127

327. SCENE IN THE TEMPLE.. 127

328. THE SCOFFERS 127

329. THE SERVANT 127

330. THE SERVANT IS TO — 128

331. SERVICE 128

332. SEVEN ASPECTS OF LOVE 128

333. SEVEN ASPECTS OF PREACHING.. 129

334. SEVEN ASPECTS OF SALVATION 129

335. SEVEN ASPECTS OF THE GOSPEL 129
336. SEVEN BLESSINGS IN PHILIPPIANS 4 130
337. SEVEN BLESSINGS IN ROMANS 5 130
338. SEVEN CHARACTERISTICS OF PHARAOH 130
339. SEVEN CHARACTERISTICS OF SAINTS 131
340. SEVEN CHARACTERISTICS OF SAINTS IN THE PSALMS 131
341. SEVEN CHARACTERISTICS OF THE PEOPLE OF GOD 131
342. SEVEN CHARACTERISTICS OF THE SHEEP 132
343. SEVEN CLASSES IN JOHN 6 132
344. SEVEN CLASSES IN PHILIPPIANS 133
345. SEVEN CLASSES IN THE DISCIPLES' PRAYER 133
346. SEVEN CLASSES OF CHILDREN 133
347. SEVEN "DAILY" THINGS 134
348. SEVEN EVERLASTING THINGS IN ISAIAH 134
349. SEVEN GIFTS 134
350. SEVEN GIFTS IN JOHN 135
351. SEVEN GOOD THINGS 135
352. SEVEN MANIFOLD THINGS 135
353. SEVEN "NOTS" IN JOHN'S GOSPEL 136
354. SEVEN POINTS IN JEREMIAH 1 136
355. SEVEN POINTS of MAN'S INSIGNIFICANCE 136
356. SEVEN STEPS IN CHRIST'S EXALTATION 137
357. SEVEN STEPS IN CHRIST'S HUMILIATION 137
358. SEVEN STEPS IN DAVID'S LIFE 138
359. SEVEN STEPS IN ISRAEL'S EXPERIENCE 138
360. SEVEN THINGS ABOUT ISRAEL 138
361. SEVEN THINGS ABOUT THE RICH MAN 139
362. SEVEN THINGS ACCOMPLISHED 139

363. SEVEN THINGS GOD DOES IN GENESIS 1	139
364. SEVEN THINGS IN 1 COR. 2	140
365. SEVEN THINGS IN PSALM 61	140
366. SEVEN THINGS OPENED	140
367. SEVEN THINGS THE BLIND MAN DID	141
368. SEVEN THINGS THE FATHER DID	141
369. SEVENFOLD PRIVILEGE IN – MATT. 6	141
370. SEVENFOLD PRIVILEGE OF THE CHILD OF GOD	142
371. A SEVENFOLD RESPONSIBILITY	142
372. A SEVENFOLD RESPONSIBILITY IN JUDE	142
373. A SEVENFOLD TESTIMONY	143
374. A SEVENFOLD VIEW OF THE LOVE OF GOD	143
375. THE SHEPHERD	143
376. SIN	144
377. SIX ASPECTS OF LIFE	144
378. SIX GOOD THINGS IN 1 TIMOTHY	144
379. SIX POINTS IN PHILIPPIANS 3	144
380. SOME NEGLECTED EXHORTATIONS	145
381. THE SONS OF ELI	145
382. THE SOUL	145
383. SPIRITUAL BLESSINGS	146
384. STAGES OF CHRISTIANITY	146
385. STRONG IN THE LORD	147
386. SUBJECTS OF DISCOURSE IN JOHN 4	147
387. SUBJECTS OF PAUL'S ADDRESS AT ATHENS	147
388. A SUM IN MULTIPLICATION	147
389. TEARS	148
390. THE TEN LEPERS	148

391. TEN STEPS IN ISRAEL'S EXPERIENCE IN THE WILDERNESS	148
392. TEN STEPS IN THE PRODIGAL'S LIFE	149
393. THERE SHALL BE SHOWERS OF BLESSING	149
394. THINGS RESERVED	149
395. THINGS THAT ARE OPENED	150
396. THINGS TO BE FULL OF	150
397. THINGS WEIGHED BY GOD	150
398. THINGS WELL PLEASING TO GOD	151
399. THOSE DELIVERED FROM CAPTIVITY WERE —	151
400. THOUGHTS FROM JOHN 17	151
401. THREE ABOMINATIONS	151
402. THREE ASPECTS OF GRACE	152
403. THREE ASPECTS OF JUDGMENT	152
404. THREE ASPECTS OF KNOWLEDGE	152
405. THREE ASPECTS OF PEACE	152
406. THREE ASPECTS OF WORK	152
407. THREE ATTITUDES OF THE BELIEVER	152
408. THREE BUNDLES	153
409. THREE CLASSES IN NUMBERS	153
410. THREE COMMANDS	153
411. THREE CONCLUSIONS	153
412. THREE CRIES	153
413. THREE CRIES FROM THREE CLASSES	153
414. THREE CUPS IN LUKE 22	154
415. THREE ENQUIRERS	154
416. THREE EXCUSES	154
417. THREE FORMS OF CORRUPTION	154
418. THREE GIFTS FROM THE FATHER TO THE SON	154

419. THREE GIFTS FROM THE LORD TO US	154
420. THREE GREAT EVENTS	155
421. THREE GREAT REALITIES IN HEBREWS	155
422. THREE HARVESTS	155
423. THREE IMPOSSIBILITIES IN HEBREWS	155
424. THREE "MUSTS" OF JOHN 3	155
425. THREE PLACES WHERE GOD PUT THE NAMES OF THE TRIBES	155
426. THREE QUESTIONS IN JEREMIAH	156
427. THREE REIGNS	156
428. THREE REPRESENTATIVE MEN	156
429. THREE SCENES	156
430. THREE STAGES In DISCIPLINE	156
431. THREE THINGS IN GENESIS 15:1	156
432. THREE THINGS IN HABAKKUK	157
433. THREE THINGS MUST BE CLEAN	157
434. THREE THINGS OPENED	157
435. THREE THINGS PROMISED TO JACOB	157
436. THREE TRUMPETS	157
437. THREEFOLD INVITATION	157
438. THREEFOLD KEEPING	158
439. THREEFOLD LOVE	158
440. THREEFOLD OBJECT OF THE LORD'S COMING	158
441. THREEFOLD REST	158
442. "TILL HE COME"	158
443. 2 TIMOTHY 3	159
444. TITLES OF CHRIST IN JOHN 1	159
445. TO HIMSELF	159
446. TOGETHER	160

447. THE TREE 160
448. THE TRINITY 160
449. TRUST IN THE LORD 160
450. TRUTHS CONNECTED WITH THE HOLY SPIRIT 161
451. TWO DESIRES 161
452. TWO MARVELS 161
453. TWO POSTAL DELIVERIES 162
454. TWO PRAYERS IN MARK 5 162
455. TWO THINGS — UNQUENCHABLE 162
456. TWOFOLD CHARGE AGAINST ISRAEL 163
457. TWOFOLD SATISFACTION 163
458. UNITED IN 163
459. UNITY 163
460. UNIVERSAL DEPRAVITY 163
461. UNSEARCHABLE RICHES 163
462. THE VALLEY 164
463. WAITING 164
464. THE WATER OF LIFE 165
465. WATER IN MOTION 165
466. WE ARE TO BE 165
467. WE SEE JESUS 166
468. WEAK THINGS 166
469. WHAT A CHILD OF GOD SHOULD HAVE 166
470. WHAT CHRIST DECLARES HIMSELF TO BE 167
471. WHAT CHRIST HAS DONE FOR US 167
472. WHAT DANIEL WAS 168
473. WHAT KIND OF MAN WAS DAVID? 168
474. WHAT IS NIGH? 168

475. WHAT JESUS DID FOR US 169

476. WHAT JONATHAN DID TO DAVID 169

477. WHAT THE LORD DOES FOR US IN PSALM 34 169

478. WHAT TO INCREASE IN: — 170

479. WHAT WE ARE 170

480. WHAT WE ARE ABLE TO DO 170

481. WHAT WE ARE NOT TO DO 171

482. WHAT WE DO BY FAITH 171

483. WHAT WE HAVE 171

484. WHAT WE OUGHT TO BE 172

485. WHAT WE OUGHT TO DO 172

486. WHAT WE RECEIVE 173

487. WHAT WE SHALL BE 173

488. WILDERNESS PROVISION in Psalm 23 173

489. WOMAN IN SIMON'S HOUSE 174

490. THE WOMAN WITH THE ISSUE OF BLOOD 175

491. THE WORD OF GOD 175

492. WORDS OF EXHORTATION 176

493. THE WORK OF CHRIST FOR ME 177

494. WORKING FOR GOD 177

495. WORTHY THINGS AND MEN 177

496. THE WRATH OF GOD 177

497. YEAR OF JUBILEE 178

498. YOUR FAITH 178

499. YOUR PATHS 178

500. ZEALOUS 178

CONCLUSION 181

1. AARON AND HIS SONS
They were CLEANSED – Lev. 8:6

They were CLOTHED – Lev. 8:7

They were GIRDED – Lev. 8:7

They were CROWNED – Lev. 8:9

They were ANOINTED – Lev. 8:12

They were SANCTIFIED – Lev. 8:30

They were CONSECRATED – Lev. 8:33

They were FED – Lev. 8:31

2. A.B.C. OF ACTS 2
ADDITION – Acts 2:41

BAPTISM – Acts 2:38,41

COMMUNION – Acts 2:42

DETERMINATION – Acts 2:42

EDIFICATION – Acts 2:42

FELLOWSHIP – Acts 2:42

GENEROSITY – Acts 2:44, 45

3. A.B.C. OF THE GOSPEL
All have sinned – Rom. 3:23

Be sure your sin will find you out – Num. 32:23

Christ died for our sins – 1 Cor. 15:3

4. ABOUNDING
In GRACE – 2 Cor. 9:8

In LOVE – Phil. 1:9

In FRUIT – Phil. 4:17

In WORK – 1 Cor. 15:58

In THANKSGIVING – Col. 2:7

In HOPE – Rom. 15:13

In CONSOLATION – 2 Cor. 1

5. ABRAHAM'S SERVANT
A PIOUS man – Gen. 24:2

A PRAYING man – Gen. 24:12

A WORSHIPPING man – Gen. 24:26

An EARNEST man – Gen. 24:33

A TRUE man (spoke of his master) – Gen. 24:35

An INDEFATIGABLE man – Gen. 24:56

6. ACCEPTABILITY
Accepted in the Beloved — STANDING – Eph. 1:6

Accepted sacrifices — WORSHIP – 1 Pet. 2:5

Acceptable to Him — SERVICE – 2 Cor. 5:9

7. ACCEPTABLE SACRIFICES
My PERSON – Rom. 12:1

My PROPERTY – Phil. 4:18

My PRAISE – Heb. 13:15

8. AFAR OFF
The PRODIGAL – Luke 15:20

The RICH MAN – Luke 16:23

The LEPERS – Luke 17:12

The PUBLICAN – Luke 18:13

PETER – Luke 22:54

9. "ALL"
All Power – Matt. 28:18

All Nations – Matt. 28:19

All Things – Matt. 28:20

All Times – Matt. 28:20

10. THE ALL'S OF COLOSSIANS
All SAINTS – Col. 1:4

All MIGHT – Col. 1:11

All PATIENCE – Col. 1:11

All TREASURES – Col. 2:3

All FULNESS – Col. 2:9

All POWER – Col. 2:10

All IN ALL (CHRIST) – Col. 3:11

All WISDOM – Col. 3:16

All THINGS (Obey) – Col. 3:22

11. ALONE
For HEALING – Mark 7:33

For SIGHT – Mark 8:23

For REVELATION – Mark 9:2

For TEACHING – Mark 4:34

For REST – Mark 6:31

12. ALWAYS

PLEASING – John 8:29

PRAYING – Acts 10:2

TRIUMPHING – 2 Cor. 2:14

MAGNIFYING – Phil. 1:20

OBEYING – Phil. 2:12

REJOICING – Phil. 4:4

REMEMBERING – 2 Pet. 1:15

13. THE AMALEKITE

I. His character —

    An Egyptian – 1 Sam. 30:11

    An enemy of David – 1 Sam. 30:14

II. His condition —

    In need – 1 Sam. 30:12

    In Sickness – 1 Sam. 30:13

    Deserted – 1 Sam. 30:13

III. To whom brought —

    David – 1 Sam. 30:11

IV. How David treated him —

    Supplied his need – 1 Sam. 30:11

    Pressed him into his Service – 1 Sam. 30:15

14. ANDREW AND HIS BROTHER

FINDING – John 1:41

TELLING – John 1:41

BRINGING – John 1:42

15. APOLLOS
He was ELOQUENT – Acts 18:24

He was MIGHTY in the Scriptures – Acts 18:24

He was FERVENT in the Spirit – Acts 18:25

He was A Diligent TEACHER – Acts 18:25

He was A Bold SPEAKER – Acts 18:26

He was A LEARNER – Acts 18:26

He was A HELPER of those who believed – Acts 18:27

16. ARISE
Arise for SERVICE – 1 Chron. 22:16

Arise for SHINING – Isa. 60:1

Arise for PILGRIMAGE – Micah 2:10

Arise for HOME – Song 2:13

17. "AS HE IS SO ARE WE"
The same FATHER – John 20:17

The same LIFE – John 14:19

The same NATURE – 2 Pet. 1:4

The same POSITION – Eph. 2:6

The same JOY – John 17:13

The same PEACE – John 14:27

The same LOVE – John 17:23

The same LIKENESS – 1 John 3:2

The same MISSION in the world – John 20:21

The same THRONE – Rev. 3:21

The same GLORY – John 17:22

18. ASPECTS OF CHRIST
The MYSTERY of Christ – Eph. 3:4

The GOSPEL of Christ – Eph. 3:6

The RICHES of Christ – Eph. 3:8

The POWER of Christ – Eph. 3:9

The PURPOSE in Christ – Eph. 3:11

The LOVE of Christ – Eph. 3:19

19. ATTITUDE OF THE BELIEVER
LOOKING – Heb. 12:2

LISTENING – Psa. 85:8

LEARNING – Matt. 11:29

LEANING – Song 8:5

LIVING – Phil. 1:21

LYING – Psa. 23:2

LOVING – 1 John 4:19

LONGING – Psa. 119:174

20. BARTIMEUS
DARKNESS — His Blindness – Mark 10:46

DESTITUTION — His Poverty – Mark 10:46

DELIVERANCE — Received his Sight – Mark 10:52

DEVOTEDNESS — Following Jesus – Mark 10:52

21. BE HOLY
Holy PRIESTHOOD – 1 Pet. 2:5

Holy WOMEN – 1 Pet. 3:5

Holy MOUNTAIN – 2 Pet. 1:18

Holy MEN – 2 Pet. 1:21

Holy COMMANDMENT – 2 Pet. 2:21

Holy PROPHETS – 2 Pet. 3:2

Holy CONVERSATION – 2 Pet. 3:11

22. THE BELIEVER
His SALVATION – Heb. 5:9

His PRESERVATION – Jude v.1

His PRESENTATION – Rom. 12:1

His PROCLAMATION – 2 Tim. 4:2

His EXCLAMATION – Zech. 9:17

His OCCUPATION – 1 Pet. 2:16

His CONSUMMATION – John 17:24

23. BELIEVERS BELONG TO CHRIST
By gift – John 6:37; 10:29; 17:6,9,11,24

By purchase – Eph. 1:14; Heb 9:12; 1 Pet 1:18-19; Gal. 3:15

By birth – John 1:12-13; James 1:18; 1 Peter 1:23; 1 John 5:1

24. THE BELIEVER'S BENEFITS
PRIVILEGE – John 17:3

SAFETY – John 17:2

DESTINY – John 17:24

25. THE BELIEVER'S CALLING

I. He who calls — God – Rom. 8:28-30

II. From what He calls — Darkness – 1 Pet. 2:9

III. To what He calls us

    Sonship – 1 John 3:1

    Saints – Rom. 1:7

    Servants – 1 Pet. 2:16

    Unity – Col. 3:15

    Fellowship – 1 Cor. 1:9

    Suffering – 1 Pet. 2:21

    Kingdom – 1 Thess. 2:12

IV. Character of the calling

    Holy – 2 Tim. 1:9

    Heavenly – Heb. 3:1

26. THE BELIEVER'S PATHWAY

A PATHWAY OF FAITH – Heb. 11:8; Phil. 4:6

A PATHWAY OF FAVOR – Psalm. 5:12

A PATHWAY OF FELLOWSHIP with Christ – 1 John 1:3; 1 Cor. 1:9

A PATHWAY OF LIGHT – Prov. 4:18; 1 John 2:9-10

A PATHWAY OF LIFE – Psalm 16:11; 1 John 3:14

A PATHWAY OF LOVE – Eph. 5:2; 1 John 2:5-6

A PATHWAY OF PEACE – Luke 1:79; Isa. 26:3

A PATHWAY OF PROGRESS – Psalm 84:7; Phil. 3:13-14

A PATHWAY OF PRIVILEGE – John 14:23; Eph. 2:18

A PATHWAY OF TRIBULATION – John 16:33

A PATHWAY OF TRUST – Isa. 50:10; Psalm 37:5

A PATHWAY OF TRIUMPH – Psalm 59:12; 1 Chron. 19:13

27. THE BELIEVER'S POSITION
GIVEN out of the world – John 17:6

SENT into the world – John 17:18

LEFT in the world – John 17:11

NOT of the world – John 17:14

HATED by the world – John 17:14

KEPT from the evil of the world – John 17:15

28. THE BELIEVER'S PRIVILEGES
LOVED by Him – Deu. 33:3

SECURED in Him – Deu. 33:3

SITTING with Him – Deu. 33:3

RECEIVING from Him – Deu. 33:3

29. BELIEVING
The PERSON to believe – Acts 16:31

The WAY to believe – Rom. 10:9

The RESULT of believing — Life – John 3:16

    Forgiveness – Acts 10:43

    Satisfaction – John 6:35

    Light – John 12:46

    Peace – Rom. 15:13

    Joy – 1 Pet. 1:8

Overcoming – 1 John 5:5

30. THE BELOVED
Accepted in the Beloved – Eph. 1:6

Opening to the Beloved – Song 5:6

Seated under the shadow of the Beloved – Song 2:3

The words of the Beloved – Song 2:10

Our estimation of the Beloved – Song 5:10

Leaning on the Beloved – Song 8:5

Bearing fruit for the Beloved – Song 4:16

Longing for the Beloved – Song 8:14

31. THE BETTER PROMISES
Eternal redemption – Heb. 9:12

Eternal salvation – Heb. 5:9

Eternal inheritance – Heb. 9:15

A better hope – Heb. 7:19

A better resurrection – Heb. 11.35

A better possession – Heb. 10.34

32. BETTER THINGS
Better THINGS of you – Heb. 6:9

Better HOPE – Heb. 7:19

Better COVENANT – Heb. 8:6

Better PROMISES – Heb. 8:6

Better COUNTRY – Heb. 11:16

Better RESURRECTION– Heb. 11:35

BLOOD of Jesus — better things, etc. – Heb. 12:24

33. BEYOND DESCRIPTION
The Unspeakable GIFT – 2 Cor. 9:15

The Unspeakable WORDS – 2 Cor. 12:4

The Unspeakable JOY – 1 Pet. 1:8

34. BLESSINGS OF THE BELIEVER
Engraved on His hands – Isa. 49:16

Enrolled in His book – Heb. 12:23

Encouraged in His service – 2 Chron. 35:2

Encamped round by His angel – Psa. 34:7

Enlightened by the Father – Eph. 1:18

Endued with power by His Spirit – Luke 24:49

35. BLESSINGS PROMISED
The Deaf shall HEAR – Isa. 29:18

The Blind shall SEE – Isa. 29:18

The Meek shall INCREASE – Isa. 29:19

The Poor shall REJOICE – Isa. 29:19

The Erring shall UNDERSTAND – Isa. 29:24

The Murmurers shall LEARN – Isa. 29:24

36. THE BODY
I must glorify God in my body – 1 Cor. 6:20

I must remember the body is not my own – 1 Cor. 6:20

I should present my body to God – Rom. 12:1

The body is the dwelling place of the Holy Spirit – 1 Cor. 6:19

I look for the time when the body will be changed – Phil. 3:21

I am to keep my body under control – 1 Cor. 9:27

37. THE BOOK
ANXIOUS for the book – Neh. 8:1

OPENING of the book – Neh. 8:5

READING the book – Neh. 8:8

UNDERSTANDING the book – Neh. 8:8

EFFECT of the book – Neh. 8:9

LOVE for the book – Neh. 8:18

OBEDIENCE to the book – Neh. 8:14-16

38. BROUGHT
Brought LOW – Psa. 116:6

Brought UP – Psa. 40:2

Brought OUT – Psa. 107:14

Brought INTO – Psa. 18:19

Brought ON – 2 Cor. 1:16

39. THE CARE OF THE SHEPHERD FOR THE SHEEP
He SEEKS them – Eze. 34:11

He DELIVERS them – Eze. 34:12

He FEEDS them – Eze. 34:14

He GATHERS them – Eze. 34:13

He STRENGTHENS them – Eze. 34:16

He RESTS them – Eze. 34:14

He PROTECTS them – Eze. 34:25

40. THE CAVE OF ADULLAM

THE PLACE —

> It was a place of safety – 1 Sam. 22:23

> It was needed – 1 Sam. 22:1

THE PEOPLE —

> Distressed – 1 Sam. 22:2

> Debtors – 1 Sam. 22:2

> Discontented – 1 Sam. 22:2

THE PERSON —

> They went to him – 1 Sam. 22:1

> He encouraged them – 1 Sam. 22:23

> He led them – 1 Sam. 22:1-5

> He fought with them – 1 Sam. 22:1-5

> He won the victory – 1 Sam. 22:1-5

41. CERTAINTIES

A sure FOUNDATION – 2 Tim. 2:19

A sure DWELLING PLACE – Isa. 32:18

A sure HOPE – Heb. 6:19

A sure CALLING – 2 Pet. 1:10

A sure WORD – 2 Pet. 1:19

A sure JUDGMENT – Rom. 2:2

A sure REWARD – Prov. 11:18

42. CHARACTERISTICS OF TRIBE OF GAD
SEPARATED men — Separated to David – 1 Chron. 12:8

POWERFUL men — Men of might – 1 Chron. 12:8

WARLIKE men — Men of War – 1 Chron. 12:8

WISE men — Handle the shield – 1 Chron. 12:8

BOLD men — Faces like lions – 1 Chron. 12:8

DILIGENT men — Swift as roes – 1 Chron. 12:8

VICTORIOUS men — Put to flight the enemy – 1 Chron. 12:15

43. THE CHILD OF GOD
Is GIVEN to Christ – John 6:37

Is DRAWN to Christ – John 6:44

Is PRESERVED by Christ – John 6:39

Is INSTRUCTED by Christ – John 6:45

Is SATISFIED by Christ – John 6:35, 57

Is RAISED by Christ – John 6:54

44. THE CHILD OF GOD SHOULD BE ABLE —
To STAND – Eph. 6:11

To WITHSTAND – Eph. 6:13

To QUENCH – Eph. 6:16

45. THE CHILD OF GOD SHOULD BE STEDFAST
In FAITH – 1 Pet. 5:9

In WORK – 1 Cor. 15:58

In LOOKING – Acts 1:10

In DOCTRINE – Acts 2:42

In MIND – Ruth 1:18

46. CHRIST'S EXPECTATIONS FOR US

Be holy (1 Peter 1:15) – For Christ is holy (1 Pet 1:16)

Be humble (1 Pet. 5:5) – For Christ was humble – (Phil. 2:8)

Be forgiving (Luke 11:4) – For Christ has forgiven (Col. 3:13)

Be patient (James 5:7) – For Christ is patient – (2 Pet. 3:15)

Be zealous (Rev. 3:19) – For Christ is zealous (Psalm 69:9)

Be prayerful (1 Thess. 5:17) – For Christ prayed (Luke 9:28)

47. CHRIST IS ALL AND IN ALL.

In Him we are—

Chosen – Eph. 1:4

Accepted – Eph. 1:6

Built together for a habitation of God through the Spirit – Eph 2:22

Blessed with all spiritual blessings (Eph. 1:3).

48. THE CHURCH SPOKEN OF

As a BODY — Unity – Eph. 1:23

As a WIFE — Love – Rev. 19:7

As a HOUSE — Stability – 1 Pet. 2:5

As a CANDLESTICK — Light – Rev. 2:1

As a FAMILY — Affection – Eph. 3:15

As a FLOCK — Care – 1 Pet. 5:2

As a PILLAR — Strength – 1 Tim. 3:15

As a PEARL — Beauty – Matt. 13:46

49. THE COMING OF THE LORD TEACHES

DELIVERANCE from idols – 1 Thess. 1:9

HAPPINESS of soul – 1 Thess. 2:19

HOLINESS of life – 1 Thess. 3:13

EXHORTING one another – 1 Thess. 4:18

BLAMELESS walk – 1 Thess. 5:23

50. THE COMMON SALVATION

Be it known to you therefore, brothers, that through this man is proclaimed to you remission of sins, and by him everyone who believes is justified from all things, from which you could not be justified by the law of Moses. – **Acts 13:38-39**

HERE IS

A Royal declaration – "proclaimed"

A purchased salvation – "through this man"

A personal salvation – "to you"

A plenteous salvation – "everyone who believes"

A present salvation – "*Is* proclaimed"

A perfect salvation – "is justified from all things"

A peerless salvation – "could not be justified by the law of Moses."

51. COMPLETE DELIVERANCE

Deliverance from all my FEARS – Psa. 34:4

Deliverance from DANGER – Psa. 34:7

Deliverance from TROUBLE – Psa. 34:17

Deliverance from AFFLICTION – Psa. 34:19

52. A CONDESCENDING GOD
The Lord looked down from heaven to see – RUIN – Psalm 14:2

The Lord looked down from heaven to hear – REPENTANCE – Psalm 102:19

The Lord looked from heaven to deliver – REDEMPTION – Psalm 33:13-19

O God, look down from heaven and visit – REVIVAL – Psalm 80:14

53. CONDITION OF THE CHURCHES
They RESTED – Acts 9:31

They were EDIFIED – Acts 9:31

They WALKED – Acts 9:31

They were COMFORTED – Acts 9:31

They were INCREASED – Acts 9:31

54. CONDITIONS TO EFFECTUAL PRAYER
Must ask in His name – John 14:14

Must ask believing – Matt. 21:22

Must ask according to His will – 1 John 5:14

Must ask in faith – James 1:6

Must abide in Him – John 15:7

55. CONQUERING POWER
He overcame the TEMPEST – Mark 4:39

He overcame the DEMONS – Mark 5:13

He overcame DISEASE – Mark 5:27, 33

He overcame DEATH – Mark 5:41-42

56. THE CONSCIENCE
A CONVICTED Conscience – John 8:9

A GOOD Conscience – Acts 23:1

A PURE Conscience – 1Tim. 3:9

A WEAK Conscience – 1 Cor. 8:10

A DEFILED Conscience – Tit. 1:15

A PURGED Conscience – Heb. 9:14

A SEARED Conscience – 1 Tim. 4:2

57. CONSIDER
Consider YOUR WAYS – Hag. 1:5

Consider HIM – Heb. 12:3

Consider NOW – Hag. 2:18

Consider YOUR END – Deu. 32:29

58. CONTINUING
Continual SAFETY – Psa. 71:3

Continual PRAISING – Psa. 71:6

Continual HOPING – Psa. 71:14

Continual PRAYING – Psa. 72:15

Continual ABIDING – Psa. 73:23

59. CONVERSATION
A HOLY conversation – 1 Pet. 1:15

A GOOD conversation – 1 Pet. 3:16

An HONEST conversation – 1 Pet. 2:12

A PURE conversation – 1 Pet. 3:2

A VAIN conversation – 1 Pet. 1:18

A DEPRAVED conversation – 2 Pet. 2:7

60. 1 CORINTHIANS 6
You were WASHED – 1 Cor. 6:11

You were JUSTIFIED – 1 Cor. 6:11

You were SANCTIFIED – 1 Cor. 6:11

You are MEMBERS – 1 Cor. 6:15

You are NOT YOUR OWN – 1 Cor. 6:19

You are BOUGHT WITH A PRICE – 1 Cor. 6:20

You are GOD'S – 1 Cor. 6:20

61. 2 CORINTHIANS 5
What we ARE — Ambassadors – 2 Cor. 5:20

What we KNOW — We have a home in heaven – 2 Cor. 5:1

    That we are confident – 2 Cor. 5:8

What we DO — We groan – 2 Cor. 5:2

    We walk – 2 Cor. 5:7

    We labor – 2 Cor. 5:9

    We please – 2 Cor. 5:6

    We persuade – 2 Cor. 5:11

What we SHALL BE — Made manifest – 2 Cor. 5:10

62. 2 CORINTHIANS 6:17-18
The Master's CALL "Come out"

The Master's COMMAND "Be separate"

The Master's PROMISE "I will receive you"

63. COUPLETS IN MATTHEW 7
Two GATES – Matt. 7:13

Two WAYS – Matt. 7:13-14

Two CLASSES – Matt. 7:13-14

Two DESTINATIONS – Matt. 7:13-14

Two TREES – Matt. 7:17-18

Two FRUITS – Matt. 7:17

Two HOUSES – Matt. 7:24-26

Two FOUNDATIONS – Matt. 7:24-26

Two BUILDERS – Matt. 7:24-26

Two RESULTS – Matt. 7:25-27

64. DAILY LIVING FOR THE CHRISTIAN
Daily searching in the Word – Acts 17:11

Daily bread from the Lord – Luke 11:3

Daily taking up the cross – Luke 9:23

Daily prayer – 1 Thess. 5:17

65. DAVID'S THREE ATTITUDES
LYING — as a penitent – 2 Sam. 12:16

SITTING — as a worshipper – 2 Sam. 7:1

STANDING — as a servant – 1 Chron. 28:2

66. DAVID'S WORKMEN
They were FIGHTING Men – 1 Chron. 27:6

They were TRUSTED Men – 1 Chron. 27:25

They were PLOUGHING Men – 1 Chron. 27:26

They were GIFTED Men – 1 Chron. 27:27

They were HIDDEN Men – 1 Chron. 27:28

They were WISE Men – 1 Chron. 27:32

They were SHEPHERDS – 1 Chron. 27:29

They were TEACHING Men – 1 Chron. 25:8

They were SINGING Men – 1 Chron. 25:7

67. DEAD WITH CHRIST
Dead to sin – Rom. 6:2

Dead to self – Rom. 6:8

Dead to the world – Gal. 6:14

Dead to the law - Rom. 7:4

68. DEUTERONOMY 31:12
Children of Israel were TO HEAR

Children of Israel were TO LEARN

Children of Israel were TO FEAR

Children of Israel were TO LOOK

Children of Israel were TO DO

69. THE DEVELOPMENT OF FAITH
No Faith – Mark 4:40

Little Faith – Luke 12:28

Great Faith – Matt. 8:10

Rich Faith – James 2:5

Precious Faith – 2 Pet. 1:1

Full Faith – Acts 6:5

Perfect Faith – James 2:22

70. THE DEVELOPMENT OF GRACE
Grace – James 4:6

Sufficient grace – 2 Cor. 12:9

Great grace – Acts 4:33

More grace – James 4:6

Abundant grace – 2 Cor. 4:15

Exceeding grace – 2 Cor. 9:14

Exceeding riches of His grace – Eph. 2:7

71. THE DEVELOPMENT OF WORKS
Dead Works – Heb. 6:1

Wicked Works – Col. 1:21

Dark Works – Rom. 13:12

Unfruitful Works – Eph. 5:11

Good Works – Matt. 5:16

Greater Works – John 14:12

Perfect Work – James 1:4

72. DOUBLE TITLES GIVEN TO THE LORD JESUS
The Author and Finisher of our faith – Heb. 12:2

The Apostle and High Priest of our profession – Heb. 3:1

The Shepherd and Overseer of our souls – 1 Pet. 2:25

73. EIGHT CHARACTERISTICS OF THE WICKED
His SUBSTANCE – Prov. 10:3

His NAME – Prov. 10:7

His MOUTH – Prov. 10:11

His FRUIT – Prov. 10:16

His HEART – Prov. 10:20

His FEAR – Prov. 10:24

His YEARS – Prov. 10:27

His EXPECTATION – Prov. 10:28

74. EIGHT CONDITIONS OF HAPPINESS

Happy is he whom God corrects – Job 5:17

Happy is he who trusts in the Lord – Prov. 16:20

Happy is he that hath mercy on the poor – Prov. 14:21

Happy is the man that fears the Lord – Prov. 28:14

Happy is he that finds wisdom – Prov. 3:13

Happy are they, who knowing His will, do it – John 13:17

Happy are you, if reproached for His name – 1 Pet. 4:14

Happy are they that endure – James 5:11

75. EIGHT CONTRASTS IN PSALM 107

One: Found no city to dwell in – Psa. 107:4

One: City of habitation – Psa. 107:7

Two: Hungry and thirsty – Psa. 107:5

Two: He satisfies – Psa. 107:9

Three: Right way – Psa. 107:7

Three: No way – Psa. 107:40

Four: Sitting in Darkness – Psa. 107:10

Four: Brought them out – Psa. 107:14

Five: Drew near to the gates of death – Psa. 107:18

Five: Declare works, etc. – Psa. 107:22

Six: The wind – Psa. 107:25

Six: The quiet – Psa. 107:30

Seven: The trouble – Psa. 107:26

Seven: Desired haven – Psa. 107:30

Eight: The storm – Psa. 107:29

Eight: The calm – Psa. 107:29

76. EIGHT THINGS ABOUT JONAH
His PRAYER – Jonah 2:1

His FAITH – Jonah 2:2

His CONFESSION – Jonah 2:4

His LOOK – Jonah 2:4

His ACKNOWLEDGEMENT – Jonah 2:6

His WORSHIP – Jonah 2:9

His DELIVERANCE – Jonah 2:10

77. EIGHT THINGS GOD DOES IN PSALM 107
He REDEEMS – Psa. 107:2

He GATHERS – Psa. 107:3

He DELIVERS – Psa. 107:6

He LEADS – Psa. 107:7

He SATISFIES – Psa. 107:9

He SAVES – Psa. 107:13

He HEALS – Psa. 107:20

He BLESSES – Psa. 107:38

78. EIGHT THINGS GOD WAS TO DAVID
ROCK – 2 Sam. 22:2

DELIVERER – 2 Sam. 22:2

FORTRESS – 2 Sam. 22:2

SHIELD – 2 Sam. 22:3

TOWER – 2 Sam. 22:3

REFUGE – 2 Sam. 22:3

SAVIOR – 2 Sam. 22:3

SALVATION – 2 Sam. 22:3

79. EIGHT THINGS IN ABUNDANCE
GRACE – 1 Tim. 1:14

PARDON – Isa. 55:7

LIFE – John 10:10

SATISFACTION – Psa. 36:8

MERCY – 1 Pet. 1:3

PEACE – Psa. 37:11

LOVE – 2 Cor. 12:15

JOY – 2 Cor. 8:2

80. EIGHT THINGS TO FIND
Finding LIFE – Prov. 8:35

Finding PASTURE – John 10:9

Finding REST – Matt. 11:29

Finding GRACE – Heb. 4:16

Finding MERCY – Hos. 14:3

Finding the GUESTS – Matt. 22:9

Finding your MESSAGE – Ecc. 12:10

Finding your WORK – Ecc. 9:10

81. EIGHTFOLD DELIVERANCE
From FEAR – Psa. 34:4

From DANGER – Psa. 34:7

Out of TROUBLE – Psa. 34:17

Out of AFFLICTIONS – Psa. 34:19

From DEATH – 2 Cor. 1:10

From the WORLD – Gal. 1:4

From DARKNESS – Col. 1:13

From WRATH – 1 Thess. 1:10

82. ENDURES FOR EVER
His RIGHTEOUSNESS – Psa. 111:3

His MERCY – Psa. 106:1

His PRAISE – Psa. 111:10

His TRUTH – Psa. 117:2

His JUDGMENTS – Psa. 119:160

His NAME – Psa. 135:13

83. ENOCH
His CHANGE – Gen. 5:22

His WALK – Gen. 5:24

His FAITH – Heb. 11:5

His OBEDIENCE – Heb. 11:5

His TRANSLATION – Heb. 11:5

His PROPHECY – Jude v.14

84. EPHESIANS 1
His GRACE – Eph. 1:6

His WILL – Eph. 1:9

His CALLING – Eph. 1:18

His INHERITANCE – Eph. 1:18

His FEET – Eph. 1:22

His BODY (the church) – Eph. 1:23

His GLORY – Eph. 1:12

His POWER – Eph. 1:19

85. EPHESIANS 2
With Christ – Eph. 2:5

Through Christ – Eph. 2:7

In Christ – Eph. 2:10

Without Christ – Eph. 2:12

86. EPHESIANS 2:13
The DISTANCE Far off

The REFUGE In Christ

The NEARNESS Made nigh

87. EPHESIANS 5:8
PAST "Sometimes darkness"

PRESENT "Now you are light"

FUTURE "Walk as children of light"

88. EPISTLE TO PHILEMON
The "FELLOW-SOLDIER" — Fighting – v.2

The "FELLOW-PRISONER" — Suffering – v.23

The "FELLOW-LABORERS" — Working – v.22

89. ETERNAL THINGS IN JUDE
Eternal LIFE — Life – v.21

Eternal CHAINS — Jude v.6

Eternal FIRE — Jude v.7

90. THE EUNUCH
Was a GREAT Man – Acts 8:27

Was a HUMBLE Man – Acts 8:31

Was an INQUIRING Man – Acts 8:34

Was a BELIEVING Man – Acts 8:37

Was a SAVED Man – Acts 8:37

Was an OBEDIENT Man – Acts 8:38

Was a REJOICING Man – Acts 8:39

91. EZRA 6
DEDICATION – Ezra 6:16

SACRIFICE – Ezra 6:17

SERVICE – Ezra 6:18

HOLINESS – Ezra 6:20

SEPARATION – Ezra 6:21

JOY – Ezra 6:22

STRENGTH – Ezra 6:22

92. FAILURE OF THE DISCIPLES
BOASTING of what they had done – Luke 9:10

WANT of sympathy with the people – Luke 9:12

UNWATCHFULNESS – Luke 9:32

UNBELIEF – Luke 9:40

DESIRE to be something – Luke 9:46

NARROWNESS of heart – Luke 9:49

NEED of patience – Luke 9:54

93. FAITH
I. What it is – Heb. 11:1

II. How it is obtained – Rom. 10:17

III. What it rests in – Col. 1:4

IV. Its Characteristics

    Obedience – Rom. 1:5

    Testimony – Rom. 1:8

    Fellowship – Rom. 1:12

    Life – Rom. 1:17

V. Its Results

    Salvation – Luke 7:50

    Justification – Rom. 5:1

    Keeping – 1 Pet. 1:5

    Protection – Eph. 6:16

    Triumph – 1 John 5:4

94. FAITH'S FUNDAMENTALS

SOURCE of it – Eph. 2:8

OBJECT of It – Heb. 12:2

GROUND of it – Rom. 10:17

RIGHTEOUSNESS of it – Rom. 4:13

UNITY of it – Eph. 4:5

TRIUMPH of it – 1 John 5:4

END of it – 1 Pet. 1:9

95. FAITH'S TRIUMPHS
In Romans 8

No CHARGE against us – 8:33

No CONDEMNATION upon us – 8:34

No EVIL happens to us – 8:28

No GOOD withholden from us – 8:32

No TRIAL to overcome us – 8:37

No POWER can separate us – 8:38-39

No COMPARISON can express the glory that awaits us – 8:18

96. FELIX

His RESPONSIBILITY – Acts 24:24

His REFUSAL – Acts 24:25

His CONDITION – Acts 24:25

His HOPE – Acts 24:26

His END – Acts 24:27

97. FELLOWSHIP
With the FATHER – 1 John 1:3

With the SON – 1 John 1:3

With the SPIRIT – Phil. 2:1

In SUFFERING – Phil. 3:10

In the GOSPEL – Phil. 1:5

With ONE ANOTHER – 1 John 1:7

In TEMPORAL THINGS – 2 Cor. 8:4

98. FIRE
REFINING Fire – Mal. 3:2

TESTING Fire – 1 Cor. 3:13

STRANGE Fire – Num. 3:4

CONSUMING Fire – Heb. 12:29

ETERNAL Fire – Jude v.7

99. FIVE ASPECTS OF CRUCIFIXION
Christ crucified for me – Gal. 3:1

I crucified with Him – Gal. 2:20

Flesh crucified in me – Gal. 5:24

World crucified to me – Gal. 6:14

I crucified to the world – Gal. 6:14

100. FIVE ASPECTS OF FRUIT-BEARING IN PAUL'S LIFE
Fruit of CONVERSION – Rom. 1:13

Fruit of HOLINESS – Rom. 6:22

Fruit of RIGHTEOUSNESS – Phil. 1:11

Fruit of GIVING – Phil. 4:17

Fruit of THANKSGIVING – Heb. 13:15

101. FIVE CLASSES
PARDON for the guilty – Neh. 9:17

PEACE for the troubled – John 14:1, 27

RECONCILIATION for enemies – 2 Cor. 5:19

REST for the weary – Matt. 11:28

HOPE for the despairing – Heb. 6:18

102. FIVE CLASSES AT THE CROSS
The WOMEN weeping – Luke 23:27

The RULERS deriding – Luke 23:35

The SOLDIERS mocking – Luke 23:36

The THIEF praying – Luke 23:42

The CENTURION glorifying – Luke 23:47

103. FIVE EXHORTATIONS IN COLOSSIANS
Let no man judge you – Col. 2:16

Let no man beguile you – Col. 2:18

Let the peace of God rule – Col. 3:15

Let the word of Christ dwell – Col. 3:16

Let your speech be always with grace – Col. 4:6

104. FIVE WAYS OF DOING THE LORD'S WORK
HEARTILY – Col. 3:23

SPEEDILY – Ezra 7:21

DILIGENTLY – Ezra 7:23

FAITHFULLY – 2 Chron. 34:12

CONTINUALLY – Dan. 6:16

105. FIVEFOLD RESULT OF HIS WORK
He has SAVED us – Eph. 2:1-5

He has RAISED us – Eph. 2:6

He has SEATED us – Eph. 2:6

He has CREATED us – Eph. 2:10

He will DISPLAY us – Eph. 2:7

106. THE FLESH
We are under no obligation to it – Rom. 8:12

We are not to make it our friend – Rom. 8:4

Not to make any allowance for it – Rom. 13:13-14

Not to let it show itself – Gal. 5:12-14

We should never trust it – Phil. 3:3-4

Expect no good from it – Gal. 5:19-21

What we are to do with it —

    Crucify it – Gal. 5:24

    Deny it – Rom. 8:13

107. FOR HIS NAME'S SAKE
HATED – Matt. 24:9

FORGIVENESS – 1 John 2:12

SERVICE – 3 John v.7

SUFFERING – Rev. 2:3

108. FORGIVENESS

The FOUNDATION of it — His Blood – Eph. 1:7

The AUTHOR of it — God – Eph. 4:32

The COMPLETENESS of it — All – Psa. 103:3

The PROCLAMATION of it — Is Preached – Acts 13:38

The RECEPTION of it — All that believe – Acts 13:39

The CERTAINTY of it — Are Forgiven – 1 John 2:12

The RESULTS of it — Saved – Luke 7:50

    Peace – Luke 7:50

    Blessed – Psa. 32:1

109. FOUR APPEARINGS

GRACE appearing – Tit. 2:11

KINDNESS appearing – Tit. 3:4

LOVE appearing – Tit. 3:4

SAVIOR appearing – Tit. 2:13

110. FOUR ASPECTS OF THE FEAST

The WORK finished – Prov. 9:1

The TABLE spread – Prov. 9:2

The GUEST invited – Prov. 9:5

The EXHORTATION given – Prov. 9:6

111. FOUR ASPECTS OF THE LORD JESUS

The CONQUEROR — "He shall divide" – Isa. 53:12

The SUBSTITUTE — "He bore the sin of many" – Isa. 53:12

The INTERCESSOR — "Made intercession" – Isa. 53:12

The JUSTIFIER — "Justify many" – Isa. 53:11

112. FOUR BLESSED STATEMENTS CONCERNING JESUS
In His Nature—Sinless – 1 Pet. 2:22

In His Life—Blameless – 1 Pet 2:23

In His Death—Vicarious – 1 Pet 2:24

In His Resurrection—Victorious – 1 Pet 3:22

113. FOUR PLACES FOR FOUR KINDS OF CHRISTIANS
A PLACE OF SECURITY FOR THOSE IN DOUBT — John 10:28

A PLACE OF STRENGTH FOR THOSE WHO ARE WEAK— Neh. 8:10

A PLACE FOR AFFECTION FOR THE TROUBLED — John 16:33

A PLACE FOR AN UNINSTRUCTED CHRISTIAN— Luke 8:35; 10:39

114. FOUR CRIES FOR MERCY
A Rich Man – Luke 16:24

A Poor Man – Luke 18:38

A Convicted Man – Luke 18:13

A Leprous Man – Luke 17:13

115. FOUR DECEITFUL THINGS
HEART – Jer. 17:9

TONGUE – Micah 6:12

RICHES – Matt. 13:22

SIN – Heb. 3:13

116. FOUR GREAT THINGS
Great LOVE – Eph. 2:4

Great SALVATION – Heb. 2:3

Great JOY – Matt. 2:10

Great WRATH – Rev. 6:17

117. FOUR HANDWRITINGS
The FIRST was on stone – Exo. 34:1

The SECOND was on plaster – Dan. 5:5

The THIRD was on wood – Matt. 27:37

The FOURTH on the heart – 2 Cor. 3:2

118. FOUR LIVELY THINGS
Lively stones – 1 Pet. 2:5

Lively oracles – Acts 7:38

Lively hope – 1 Pet. 1:3

Lively enemies – Psalm 38:19

119. FOUR MANIFESTATIONS OF THE LORD
To MARY — the sorrowing one – John 20:11-16

To the DISCIPLES — the troubled ones – John 20:19-21

To THOMAS — the unbelieving one – John 20:24-28

To all the DISCIPLES — the disappointed ones – John 21:1-6

120. FOUR MEN IN LUKE 5
A troubled man calmed – Luke 5:10

A defiled man cleansed – Luke 5:12-13

A palsied man healed – Luke 5:24-25

A rich man satisfied – Luke 5:27-29

121. FOUR P's IN PSALM 42

David panting – v. 1

David pouring – v. 4

David pouting – v. 5

David praising – v. 11

122. FOUR POURINGS OUT

The BLOOD – Lev. 4:7

The BLESSING – Mal. 3:10

The SPIRIT – Acts 2:17, 18

The WRATH – Rev. 14:10

123. FOUR QUESTIONS PUT TO JONAH

What are you doing? – Jonah 1:8

Where do you come from? – Jonah 1:8

Where are you going? – Jonah 1:8

To whom do you belong? – Jonah 1:8

124. FOUR "REMEMBERS"

Remember how far you have fallen (the backslider) – Rev. 2:5

Remember now your Creator (the young) – Ecc. 12:1

Remember Lot's wife (the careless) – Luke 17:32

Son, remember (the religious) – Luke 16:25

125. FOUR SNARES TO WATCH AGAINST

INDIFFERENCE — My Lord is delayed – Matt. 24:48

NEGLIGENCE — No oil – Matt. 25:3

SELF-RIGHTEOUSNESS — When did we see you? etc. – Matt. 25:44

INDOLENCE — Hid my talent – Matt. 25:25

126. FOUR STEPS
My STANDING — In Him – Phil. 3:9

My OBJECT — Know Him – Phil. 3:10

My HOPE — Be with Him – Phil. 1:23

My PRIVILEGE — Rejoice in Him – Phil. 4:4

127. THE FOUR SUPPERS
The supper of GRACE – Luke 14:16

The supper of REMEMBRANCE – Luke 22:19-20

The supper of JOY – Rev. 19:9

The supper of WRATH – Rev. 19:17

128. FOUR THINGS ABOUT JONAH
He was DISOBEDIENT – Jonah 1:2-3

He PRAYED – Jonah 2:1

He OBEYED – Jonah 3:2-3

He was ANGRY – Jonah 4:2

129. FOUR THINGS GOD DOES FOR ME
He FINDS me – Deu. 32:10

He LEADS me – Deu. 32:10

He INSTRUCTS me – Deu. 32:10

He KEEPS me – Deu. 32:10

130. FOUR THINGS GOD PREPARED FOR JONAH
Prepared a FISH – Jonah 1:17

Prepared a GOURD – Jonah 4:6

Prepared a WORM – Jonah 4:7

Prepared an EAST WIND – Jonah 4:8

131. FOUR THINGS MEN LOVE
MONEY – 1 Tim. 6:10

WORLD – 2 Tim. 4:10

SELF – 2 Tim. 3:2

PLEASURE – 2 Tim. 3:4

132. FOUR THINGS SAID OF THE UNSAVED
They KNOW not – 2 Thess. 1:8

They OBEY not – 2 Thess. 1:8

They RECEIVE not – 2 Thess. 2:10

They BELIEVE not – 2 Thess. 2:12

133. FOUR THOUGHTS ABOUT ISRAEL
A people redeemed from death – Exo. 12:13

A people separated from Egypt – Exo. 12:51

A people journeys to Canaan – Exo. 12:11

A people dependent on the Lord – Exo. 12:23

134. FOURFOLD ASPECT OF THE WORD
The Word GIVEN – John 17:8

The Word RECEIVED – John 17:8

The Word KEPT – John 17:6

The Word SANCTIFYING – John 17:17

135. FOURFOLD DESCRIPTION OF OURSELVES
We were Dead in Trespasses and Sins – Eph. 2:1

We Walked according to the Course of this World – Eph. 2:2

We Fulfilled the Desires of the Flesh and Mind – Eph. 2:3

Were by Nature the Children of Wrath – Eph. 2:3

136. FOURFOLD VIEW OF GOD
God in MERCY – Eph. 2:4

God in LOVE – Eph. 2:4

God in GRACE – Eph. 2:5

God in KINDNESS – Eph. 2:7

137. FOURFOLD WITNESSING
JOHN the Baptist – John 5:33

The WORKS – John 5:36

The FATHER – John 5:37

The SCRIPTURES – John 5:39

138. FRUIT BEARING
Fruit of the old man – Rom. 6:21

Fruit of the new man – Rom. 6:22

Fruit God expects – Rom. 1:13; – Phil. 4:17

Fruit-bearing — a mark of God's children – Matt. 7:16

Secret of fruit-bearing – John 15:4

Hindrances to fruit-bearing – Matt. 13:22

Fruit-bearing — progressive – Mark 4:28-29

Fruit-bearing — result of Christ's death – John 12:24

139. GENESIS 1
CONVERSION — From darkness to light – Gen. 1:2-3

SEPARATION — Dividing light from darkness – Gen. 1:7

FRUIT BEARING — Tree yielding fruit – Gen. 1:12

140. GIDEON
Secret of his SUCCESS – Judges 6:12

His UNBELIEF – Judges 6:13

His POWER – Judges 6:14

His COMMISSION – Judges 6:14

His WORSHIP – Judges 6:24

His OBEDIENCE – Judges 6:27

His TRIAL – Judges 6:30

His SERVICE

    At Home – Judges 6:25

    Abroad – Judges 7:16

His VICTORY – Judges 7:20-23

His HUMILITY – Judges 8:2-3

His TEMPTATION – Judges 8:22-26

His DEFEAT – Judges 8:27

141. GIFTS FROM THE LORD
The Lord blessed me abundantly – Jos. 17:14

The Lord has helped us – 1 Sam. 7:12

The Lord has brought me – 2 Sam. 7:18

142. GLORY
The God of Glory – Acts 7:2

The Father of Glory – Eph. 1:17

The Lord of Glory 1 Cor. 2:8

The Spirit of Glory – 1 Pet. 4:14

The weight of Glory – 2 Cor. 4:17

The hope of Glory – Col. 1:27

The crown of Glory – 1 Pet. 5:4

143. GOD
The GOSPEL of God – Rom. 1:1

The SON of God – Rom. 1:4

The WILL of God – Rom. 1:10

The POWER of God – Rom. 1:16

The RIGHTEOUSNESS of God – Rom. 1:17

The WRATH of God – Rom. 1:18

The JUDGMENT of God – Rom. 1:32

144. GOD'S CAUTIONS
Beware lest you forget God – Deu. 6:12

Beware of wicked thoughts – Deu. 15:9

Beware lest He take you away – Job 36:18

Beware of leaven – Luke 12:1

Beware of covetousness – Luke 12:15

Beware lest any man spoil you – Col. 2:8

Beware of being led away – 2 Pet. 3:17

145. GOD'S FAITHFULNESS TO ISRAEL

I have LOVED – Jer. 31:3

I will GATHER – Jer. 31:8

I will LEAD – Jer. 31:9

I have REDEEMED – Jer. 31:11

I will SATISFY – Jer. 31:14

I will WATCH over – Jer. 31:28

I will FORGIVE – Jer. 31:34

146. GOD'S GRACE SHOWN TO ISRAEL

God's dealing with them in the past —

REDEEMED them – Jer. 31:11

REMEMBERED them – Jer. 31:20

LOVED them – Jer. 31:3

DREW them – Jer. 31:3

God's promise to them in the future —

He will FORGIVE them – Jer. 31:34

He will FORGET their sin – Jer. 31:34

He will GATHER them out – Jer. 31:8

He will KEEP them near – Jer. 31:10

He will LEAD them on – Jer. 31:9

He will PROSPER them in the way – Jer. 31:12

He will SATISFY them fully – Jer. 31:14

He will WATCH over them continually – Jer. 31:28

147. GOD'S "I WILL"
In Exodus 25:22

"I will meet" – The Divine meeting

"I will commune" – The Divine communing

"I will give" – The Divine giving

148. GOD'S INTEREST IN HIS PEOPLE
God DWELLING with His people – Zep. 3:17

God DELIVERING His people – Zep. 3:17

God DELIGHTING in His people – Zep. 3:17

149. GOD'S PURPOSE IN CHASTENING
For PROVING – Deu. 8:2, 3

For PURIFYING – Mal. 3:3

For TEACHING – Psa. 119:71

For HUMBLING – 2 Cor. 12:7

For RESTORING – Psa. 119:67

For PROMOTION – Dan. 3:23, 30

150. GOD'S THREE APPOINTMENTS
SALVATION – 1 Thess. 5:9

DEATH – Heb. 9:27

JUDGMENT – Acts 17:31

151. GOD'S THREE FINDINGS
He found him in a desert land – Deu. 32:10

He found a ransom – Job 33:24

Weighed and found wanting – Dan. 5:27

152. GOOD WORKS

Adorned with good works – 1 Tim. 2:9-10

Reported for good works – 1 Tim. 5:10

Rich in good works – 1 Tim. 6:18

Furnished to all good works – 2 Tim. 3:17

A pattern of good works – Tit. 2:7

Zealous of good works – Tit. 2:14

Maintain good works – Tit. 3:8

153. THE GOSPEL IN JOB 33

Man's Course — Going down – v.24

Man's Condition — Asleep – v.15

God's Attitude — Gracious – v.24

God's Provision — an Atonement – v.24

God's Message — Deliver him – Job v.24

154. GRACE

I. Its source – 1 Tim. 1:2

II. Its channel – John 1:17

III. Its Character

    Abounding – 2 Cor. 9:8

    Rich – Eph. 1:7

    Abundant – 1 Tim. 1:14

    Sufficient – 2 Cor. 12:9

    Glorious – Eph. 1:6

IV. Subjects

      The Sinner – 1 Tim. 1:14, 15

      The Saint – Eph. 3:8

      Humble – 1 Pet. 5:5

V. Its Results

      I am called – Gal. 1:15

      I am Saved – Eph. 2:5

      I am Justified – Rom. 3:24

      I Serve – Heb. 12:28

      I Hope – 2 Thess. 2:16

155. THE GRIEVOUS ESTATE OF THE WICKED

No fear of God before his eyes – Psa. 36:1

Flatters himself in his own eyes – Psa. 36:2

The words of his mouth are iniquity and deceit – Psa. 36:3

Fails to act wisely – Psa. 36:3

He devises mischief upon his bed – Psa. 36:4

He sets himself in a way that is not good – Psa. 36:4

He does not abhor evil – Psa. 36:4

156. THE GROWTH OF THE BELIEVER

SECRET of the Growth – 1 Pet. 2:2

WHERE to Grow – Eph. 4:15

HOW to Grow – Psa. 92:12

WHAT to Grow in

      Grace – 2 Pet. 3:18

      Knowledge – 2 Pet. 3:18

Faith – 2 Thess. 1:3

157. HE IS ABLE
What the Lord Jesus Christ is able to do for us

Save to the uttermost – Heb. 7:25

Keep from falling – Jude v. 24

Build up – Acts 20:32

Make stand – Rom. 14:4

Aid those tempted – Heb. 2:18

Subdue all things – Phil. 3:21

Make grace abound – 2 Cor. 9:8

Exceeding abundantly above all we ask – Ephesians 3.20

158. HE KNOWS
Them that are His – 2 Tim. 2:19

The way of the righteous – Psa. 1:6

Our hearts – Luke 16:15

Our frame – Psa. 103:14

Them that trust in Him – Nah. 1:7

What we need – Matt. 6:8

How to deliver the godly – 2 Pet. 2:9

159. HEAVENLY PLACES
BLESSINGS – Eph. 1:3

POWER – Eph. 1:20

UNION – Eph. 2:6

REST – Eph. 2:6

TESTIMONY – Eph. 3:10

CONFLICT – Eph. 6:12

160. THE HEBREW CAPTIVES
They were BELIEVING men – Dan. 3:28

They were PROTECTED men – Dan. 3:27

They were DELIVERED men – Dan. 3:17

They were CONSECRATED men – Dan. 3:28

They were FEARLESS men – Dan. 3:12

They were PRIVILEGED men – Dan. 3:25

They were PROMOTED men – Dan. 3:30

161. HELP
I. The Helper – Psa. 37:40

II. WHOM He helps —

    The helpless – Job 29:12

    The Fatherless – Job 29:12

    The Low – Psa. 116:6

III. WHEN He helps —

    In time of trouble – Psa. 46:1

    In time of need – Heb. 4:16

IV. RESULT of being helped —

    Happiness – Psa. 146:5

    Continuance – Acts 26:22

    Confidence – Heb. 13:6

162. "HIS"

His CHAMBERS – Song 1:4

His TABLE – Song 1:12

His SHADOW – Song 2:3

His GARDEN – Song 4:16

His FRUIT – Song 2:3

His BANNER – Song 2:4

His HANDS – Song 2:6

His HEART – Song 3:11

163. HIS GLORY

All things created by Him – Col. 1:16

All things created for Him – Col. 1:16

All things consist by Him – Col. 1:17

All things after Him – Col. 1:17

All things beneath Him – Col. 1:18

All fulness dwelling in Him – Col. 1:19

All things reconciled by Him – Col. 1:20

164. HIS KINGDOM

The GLORY of it – Psa. 145:11

The MAJESTY of it – Psa. 145:12

The DURATION of it – Psa. 145:13

165. HIS PRESENCE

In His presence I have SALVATION – Psa. 42:5

In His presence I have REST – Exo. 33:14

In His presence I have JOY – Psa. 16:11

In His presence I have SAFETY – Psa. 31:20

In His presence I have highest COMMUNION – Psa. 140:13; – Song 2:14

166. HIS VOICE
The Voice of a PHYSICIAN – John 5:6

The Voice of a SAVIOR – Matt. 11:28

The Voice of a TEACHER – Matt. 11:29

The Voice of a SHEPHERD – John 10:4

The Voice of a MASTER – Luke 19:13

The Voice of a BELOVED – Song 2:8

The Voice of a JUDGE – John 5:25-27

167. HIS WINGS
A place of REFUGE – Psa. 17:8

A place of CONFIDENCE – Psa. 36:7

A place of REJOICING – Psa. 63:7

A place of HEALING – Mal. 4:2

A place of DELIVERANCE – Exo. 19:4

168. HOLY BOLDNESS
Boldness in APPROACHING – Heb. 4:16

Boldness in ENTERING – Heb. 10:19

Boldness in SAYING – Heb. 13:6

169. THE HOLY SPIRIT IN EPHESIANS
Sealed by the Spirit – 1:13

Accepted by the Spirit – 2:18

Habitation through the Spirit – 2:22

Revelation by the Spirit – 3:5

Strengthened by the Spirit – 3:16

Grieve not the Spirit – 4:30

Filled with the Spirit – 5:18

Sword of the Spirit – 6:17

Praying in the Spirit – 6:18

170. THE HOPE
A LIVING hope – 1 Pet. 1:3

A GOOD hope – 2 Thess. 2:16

A BLESSED hope – Tit. 2:13

A SURE hope – Heb. 6:19

A JOYFUL hope – 1 Thess. 2:19

A PURYFYING hope – 1 John 3:3

171. THE HOPE IN COLOSSIANS
Hope of the GOSPEL – Col. 1:23

Hope of GLORY – Col. 1:27

Hope laid up in HEAVEN – Col. 1:5

172. HOSEA 14
They shall GROW – v.5

They shall SPREAD – v.6

They shall BE FRUITFUL – v.7

They shall RETURN – v.7

They shall REVIVE – v.7

They shall UNDERSTAND – v.9

They shall KNOW – v.9

They shall WALK – v.9

173. HOW BOAZ DEALT WITH RUTH
He SPOKE to her – Ruth 2:8

He REFRESHED her – Ruth 2:14

He CARED for her – Ruth 2:15, 16

He ENCOURAGED her – Ruth 3:11

He GAVE to her – Ruth 3:15

He PURCHASED her – Ruth 4:10

He was UNITED to her – Ruth 4:10

174. HOW LONG?
How long do I have to live? – 2 Sam. 19:34

How long will you waver between two opinions? – 1 Kings 18:21

How long until they believe? – Num. 14:11

How long will you sleep? – Prov. 6:9

How long will you refuse to humble yourself? – Exo. 10:3

175. IMPORTANT QUESTION AND ANSWER
Who shall be able to stand? – Rev. 6:17

They stood before the throne – Rev. 7:9

176. IN A MOMENT
Affliction is for a moment – 2 Cor. 4:17

Refreshing every moment – Isa. 27:3

Death is in a moment – Job 34:20

Changed in a moment – 1 Cor. 15:52

Joy of the unsaved is for a moment – Job 20:5

Judgment will come in a moment – Lam. 4:6

177. IN JEREMIAH WE HAVE
INSPIRATION — Your words – Jer. 15:16

SEARCHING — found – Jer. 15:16

SATISFACTION — eat them – Jer. 15:16

REJOICING — the joy – Jer. 15:16

PRIVILEGE — called – Jer. 15:16

SEPARATION — never sat – Jer. 15:17

TESTIMONY — sat alone – Jer. 15:17

178. "IN LOVE"
Before Him in love – Eph. 1:4

Rooted and grounded in love – Eph. 3:17

Forbearing one another in love – Eph. 4:2

Speaking the truth in love – Eph. 4:15

Edifying the body in love – Eph. 4:16

Walking in love – Eph. 5:2

179. IN PHILIPPIANS 4, WE HAVE
An EXHORTATION – v.4

A COMMAND – v.6

A SWEET PRIVILEGE – v.6

A BLESSED PROMISE – v.7

A LIFE LESSON – v.11

The SECRET of POWER – v.13

COMPLETE SATISFACTION – v.18

UNLIMITED SUPPLY – v.19

180. "IN THE LORD"
BRETHREN in the Lord – Phil. 1:14

HOPING (R.V.) in the Lord – Phil. 2:19

TRUSTING in the Lord – Phil. 2:24

RECEIVING in the Lord – Phil. 2:29

REJOICING in the Lord – Phil. 3:1

STANDING in the Lord – Phil. 4:1

SAME MIND in the Lord – Phil. 4:2

181. THE INHERITANCE
HOW it is obtained — by birth – 1 Pet. 1:3

The BEAUTY of it — incorruptible – 1 Pet. 1:4

The PERFECTION of it — undefiled – 1 Pet. 1:4

The CERTAINTY of it — reserved – 1 Pet. 1:4

The DURATION of it — eternal – Heb. 9:15

182. ISAIAH IN THE TEMPLE
The VISION he saw – Isa. 6:1

The POSITION he was in – Isa. 6:5

The CONFESSION he made – Isa. 6:5

The INIQUITY removed – Isa. 6:7

The VOICE he heard – Isa. 6:8

The COMMAND received – Isa. 6:9

183. ISAIAH 55:1-2

THIRSTY ones

POOR ones

SQUANDERING ones

DISSATISFIED ones

184. ISAIAH 57:19-20

We have — A PROCLAMATION OF PEACE

We have — A PROMISE OF HEALTH

We have — A PICTURE OF THE WICKED

185. ISRAEL BROUGHT OUT OF CAPTIVITY

They were DELIVERED ones – Ezra 6:21

They were SEPARATED ones – Ezra 6:21

They were PRIVILEGED ones – Ezra 6:21

They were OBEDIENT ones – Ezra 6:22

They were JOYFUL ones – Ezra 6:22

They were STRENGTHENED ones – Ezra 6:22

They were WORKING ones – Ezra 6:22

186. ISRAEL IN THE WILDERNESS

Israel's POSITION – Exo. 17:1

Israel's CONDITION – Exo. 17:3

Israel's PROVISION – Exo. 17:6

Israel's CONFLICT – Exo. 17:8

Israel's VICTORY – Exo. 17:13

Israel's WORSHIP – Exo. 17:15

187. JEHOIAKIM

His captivity — The cause of it – 2 Chron. 36:5

The duration of it – Jer. 52:31

His deliverance — Lifted him up – Jer. 52:31

Brought out of prison – Jer. 52:31

The message he heard — Spoke good things – Jer. 52:32

The way he was cared for — He was enthroned – Jer. 52:32

He was clothed – Jer. 52:33

He was fed – Jer. 52:33

He was continually thought of – Jer. 52:34

188. JEREMIAH A SERVANT

Divine COMMISSION – Jer. 1:7

Divine AUTHORITY – Jer. 1:7

Divine PRESENCE – Jer. 1:8

Divine DELIVERANCE – Jer. 1:8

Divine POWER – Jer. 1:9

Divine MESSAGE – Jer. 1:9

Divine RESULT – Jer. 1:10

189. JESUS

The Person to be OBEYED – John 2:5

The Person to be TRUSTED – 2 Tim. 1:12

The Person to be LOVED – 1 John 4:19

The Person to be PROCLAIMED – 1 Cor. 1:23

The Person to be EXALTED – Isa. 52:13; – Phil. 2:9

The Person to be PLEASED – 1 John 3:22

The Person to be EXPECTED – Phil. 3:20

190. JOB 36:18
The actual — "Because there is wrath"

The probable — "Lest He take you away"

The impossible — "A great ransom" etc.

191. JOHN 11:28-29
The COMING

The CALLING

The RESPONDING

192. JOHN 14
The Father's HOUSE – v.2

The Father's WORKS – v.10

The Father's GLORY – v.13

The Father's GIFT – v.16

The Father's LOVE – v.21

The Father's PRESENCE – v.23

The Father's WORD – John v.24

193. JOHN'S FOUR-FOLD ATTITUDE
LEANING on Jesus – John 13:23

STANDING by His cross – John 19:26

RUNNING to His tomb – John 20:4

FOLLOWING his risen Lord – John 21:20

194. JOINED UNTO THE LORD

IN FELLOWSHIP – Called unto the fellowship of His dear Son – 1 Cor. 1:9; 1 John 1:3

IN SERVICE – Apart from me you can do nothing (John 15:5). As the Lord Jesus relied on the Father (John 5:19), so we must rely on Him (John 15:4). He that is joined unto the Lord is one Spirit (1 Cor. 6:17)

195. JONAH ON THE DOWN GRADE

Went down to Joppa – Jonah 1:3

Went down to the ship – Jonah 1:3

Went down into the sea – Jonah 2:6

196. JONAH'S MESSAGE

I. Character of message proclaimed —

    Judgment – Jonah 3:4

II. Effect produced by the message —

    Faith – Jonah 3:5

    Humility – Jonah 3:5

    Earnestness – Jonah 3:8

    Repentance – Jonah 3:8

III. Inquiry awakened by the message —

    Anxiety – Jonah 3:9

    Desire to be saved – Jonah 3:9

197. JOSEPH AND HIS BRETHREN

They were afraid of him – Gen. 45:3

They were at a distance from him – Gen. 45:4

They had sold him – Gen. 45:4

He loves them – Gen. 45:2

He invites them to him – Gen. 45:4

He proclaims life to them – Gen. 45:5

He promises them a great deliverance – Gen. 45:7

198. JOSEPH AND JESUS

Joseph, the SHEPHERD – Gen. 49:24

Joseph, STRIPPED – Gen. 37:23

Joseph, SOLD – Gen. 37:28

Joseph, In the PIT – Gen. 37:24

Joseph, FALSELY ACCUSED – Gen. 39:14

Joseph, In PRISON – Gen. 39:20

Joseph, HATED – Gen. 37:4

Joseph, WEPT – Gen. 50:17

Joseph, RAISED to the highest place in Egypt – Gen. 41:40

(COMPARE)

Jesus, the GOOD SHEPHERD – John 10:11

Jesus, STRIPPED – Matt. 27:28

Jesus, SOLD – Matt. 26:15

Jesus, In the PIT – Psa. 88:4

Jesus, FALSELY ACCUSED – Mark 14:56-57

Jesus, In PRISON – Isa. 53:8

Jesus, HATED – John 15:24

Jesus, WEPT – John 11:35

Jesus, RAISED to highest place in Glory – Eph. 1:20-21

199. JOTTINGS FROM PSALM 145

What the LORD IS —

    Great – v.3

    Gracious – v.8

    Merciful – v.8

    Good – v.9

    Righteous – v.17

    Nigh – v.18

What the LORD DOES —

    He Upholds – v.14

    He Gives – v.15

    He Satisfies – v.16

    He Fulfils – v.19

    He Saves – v.19

    He Hears – v.19

    He Keeps – v.20

What WE DO — We Speak of

    His Honor – v.5

    His Works – v.5

    His Acts – v.6

    His Greatness – v.6

    His Goodness – v.7

    His Glory – v.11

    His Power – v.11

200. JOY
SOURCE of Joy – Psa. 43:4

SACRIFICES of Joy – Psa. 27:6

FULNESS of Joy – 1 John 1:4

UNSPEAKABLE Joy – 1 Pet. 1:8

EXCEEDING Joy – Jude v.24

GREAT Joy – Luke 24:52

EVERLASTING Joy – Isa. 35:10

201. THE JUDGMENT
The THRONE – Rev. 20:11

The JUDGE – Rev. 20:11

The PERSONS – Rev. 20:12

The BOOKS – Rev. 20:12

The SENTENCE – Rev. 20:15

202. JUSTIFICATION DEFINED
WHAT it is – Rom. 4:5-8

The ONE who justifies – Rom. 8:33

WHOM He justifies – Rom. 4:5

HOW he is justified – Rom. 3:24; – Rom. 5:9

From WHAT he is justified – Acts 13:39

RESULT of being justified – Rom. 5:1

203. JUSTIFICATION, OUR NEED FOR IT
We are UNGODLY – Rom. 5:6

We are WITHOUT STRENGTH – Rom. 5:6

We are SINNERS – Rom. 5:8

We are ENEMIES – Rom. 5:10

204. JUSTIFICATION, OUR SOURCE
The AUTHOR — God – Rom. 8:33

The SPRING — Grace – Rom. 3:24

The GROUND — Blood – Rom. 5:9

The PROOF — Resurrection – Rom. 4:25

The PRINCIPAL — Faith – Rom. 5:1

The RESULT — Peace – Rom. 5:1

205. THE KING
The ORDER of the King – 1 Chron. 25:2

The HANDS of the King – 1 Chron. 25:6

The SERVICE of the King – 1 Chron. 26:30

The INTERESTS of the King – 1 Chron. 26:32

The ARMY of the King – 1 Chron. 27:34

The TREASURES of the King – 1 Chron. 26:26

The VOICE of the King – 1 Chron. 28:2

SUBMISSION to the King – 1 Chron. 29:24

206. THE LAMB
WORK of the Lamb – John 1:29

WALK of the Lamb – John 1:36

WORSHIP of the Lamb – Rev. 5:8-13

BLOOD of the Lamb – Rev. 7:14

WRATH of the Lamb – Rev. 6:16

MARRIAGE of the Lamb – Rev. 19:9

VICTORY of the Lamb – Rev. 17:14

207. LAZARUS
He was DEAD – John 11:14

He was CORRUPT – John 11:39

He was RAISED TO LIFE – John 11:44

He had LIBERTY – John 11:44

He had COMMUNION – John 12:2

He gave TESTIMONY – John 12:11

208. LESSONS FROM LOT'S WIFE
Her position — In a doomed city – Gen. 19:13

She was the subject of prayer – Gen. 18

She was the object of divine care – Gen. 19:15-22

She was warned by the angels – Gen. 19:12-14

She lingered with her husband – Gen. 19:16

She looked back – Gen. 19:26

She perished – Gen. 19:26

209. LESSONS FROM LUKE 5
FAILURE — "Have taken nothing" – Luke 5:5

FAITH — "At Your word" – Luke 5:5

FULNESS — "Great multitude of fishes" – Luke 5:6

FELLOWSHIP — "Beckoned unto their partners" – Luke 5:7

FISHING — "You shall catch men" – Luke 5:10

FORSAKING — "Forsook all" – Luke 5:11

FOLLOWING — "Followed Him" – Luke 5:11

210. LESSONS FROM RUTH 3
Ruth's PREPARATION — Washing – v.3

    Anointing – v.3

    Clothing – v.3

Ruth's OBEDIENCE – v.5

Ruth's POSITION — At his feet – v.14

211. LESSONS FROM THE AXE HEAD
It was lost – 2 Kings 6:5

It was in a place of death – 2 Kings 6:4-5

It had to be accounted for (borrowed) – 2 Kings 6:5

It was recovered – 2 Kings 6:6-7

The means used — branch cut down – 2 Kings 6:6; – Isa. 11:1

Person who recovered it — man of God – 2 Kings 6:6

212. LESSONS FROM THE PLAGUE OF HAIL
The CERTAINTY of the Judgment – Exo. 9:18

The SEVERITY of it – Exo. 9:18

The TIME to escape it – Exo. 9:19

The WAY of escape open to all – Exo. 9:19

The only place of SHELTER – Exo. 9:19

The only place free from JUDGMENT – Exo. 9:26

213. LITTLE THINGS WITH GREAT RESULTS
A little CLOUD – 1 Kings 18:44

A little MAID – 2 Kings 5:2

A little FOX – Song 2:15

A little MEMBER – James 3:5

A little WHILE – Heb. 10:37

214. THE LIVING BREAD
It SAVES – John 6

It SATISFIES – John 6

It STRENGTHENS – John 6

215. LOOKING
WHOM to look to – Heb. 12:2

WHOM to look for – Phil. 3:20

WHEN to look – Gen. 15:5

WHERE to look – Psa. 5:3

HOW to look — Diligently – Heb. 12:15

    Steadfastly – Acts 7:55

    Result of looking — Saved – Isa. 45:22

    Rewarded – 2 John 1:8

216. THE LORD IS READY
To PARDON – Neh. 9:17

To SAVE – Isa. 38:20

To FORGIVE – Psa. 86:5

To JUDGE – 1 Pet. 4:5

217. THE LORD JESUS AND HIS PEOPLE
HE has died, – Rom. 6:10

    So have we, – Rom. 6:11

HE has risen, – Rom. 4:25

    So have we, – Col. 2:12

HE is in heavenly places, – Eph. 1:20

    So are we, – Eph. 2:6

HE is perfected, – Heb. 5:9

    So are we, – Heb. 10:14

HE is in the Father's love, – John 5:20

    So are we, – John 17:23

HE is expecting, – Heb. 10:13

    So are we, – Phil. 3:20

HE will reign, – 1 Cor. 15:25

    So shall we, – Rev. 22:5

218. THE LORD JESUS IN MARK 1

As the OBEDIENT one – v.9

As the HUMBLE one – v.9

As the APPROVED one – v.11

As the TEMPTED one – v.13

As the WORKING one – v.14

As the GATHERING one – v.17

As the TEACHING one – v.21

219. THE LORD JESUS IN PSALM 16

His DEPENDENCE – v.1

His SUBJECTION – v.2

His FELLOWSHIP – v.3

His FIDELITY – v.4

His PORTION – v.5

His SATISFACTION – v.6

His DEVOTEDNESS – v.8

His GLORY – v.9

220. THE LORD'S RETURN
LOOKING for His return – Phil. 3:20

HASTENING His return – 2 Pet. 3:12

PRAYING for His return – Rev. 22:20

OCCUPYING till His return – Luke 19:13

WAITING for His return – Matt. 25:13

WATCHING for His return – 1 Cor. 1:7

LOVING His return – 2 Tim. 4:8

221. LOVE
TOWARDS us – 1 John 4:9

IN us – 1 John 4:12

TO us – 1 John 4:16

WITH us – 1 John 4:17

222. LOVE'S ADVANTAGES
REST of love – John 13:23

CONFIDENCE of love – John 13:25

OBEDIENCE of love – John 19:26-27

ACTIVITY of love – John 20:4

Close COMPANIONSHIP of love – John 21:20

WHOM to love — All saints – Col. 1:4

CHARACTER of the love — In the Spirit – Col. 1:8

EFFECT of the love — Hearts knit together – Col. 2:2

223. LOVED ONES IN GOSPEL OF JOHN
The WORLD – John 3:16

MARTHA – John 11:5

MARY – John 11:5

LAZARUS – John 11:5

HIS OWN – John 13:1

LOVED YOU – John 15:9

DISCIPLE – John 21:20

224. LOVE'S SACRIFICE
Ruth left all – Ruth 2:11

Jonathan gave all – 1 Sam. 18:4

Three mighty men risked all – 2 Sam. 23:16

225. LUKE 23:33
The PLACE — "There"

The AGENTS — "They"

The ACT — "Crucified"

The VICTIM — "Him"

226. MADE

The Lord Jesus (the Word) *made* all things – John 1:3

By Him also He (God) *made* the worlds – Heb. 1:2

By Him were all things created that are in heaven and that are in earth . . . all things were created for Him and by Him – Col. 1:16

But to provide salvation He was

Made flesh – John 1:14

Made of a woman – Gal. 4:4

Made of the seed of David – Rom. 1:3

Made in the likeness of man – Phil. 2:7

Made of no reputation – Phil. 2:7

Made lower than angels – Heb. 2:7

Made under the law – Gal. 4:4

Made a curse for us – Gal. 3:13

Made to be sin for us – 2 Cor. 5:21

After Resurrection He was

Made both Lord and Christ – Acts 2:36

Made so much better than angels – Heb. 1:4

Made surety of a better testament – Heb. 7:22

Made a priest . . . after the power of an endless life – Heb. 7:15-16

Made the cornerstone – 1 Pet. 2:7

Made most blessed forever – Psa. 21:6

227. MAN

His CONDITION described – Gen. 6:5

A SENTENCE pronounced – Gen. 6:13

A REFUGE provided – Gen. 6:14

An INVITATION given – Gen. 7:1

A WARNING uttered – Gen. 7:4

SALVATION accepted – Gen. 7:7

SAFETY secured – Gen. 7:16

228. THE MAN IN EPHESIANS

The NEW Man – Eph. 2:15

The INNER Man – Eph. 3:16

The PERFECT Man – Eph. 4:13

The OLD Man – Eph. 4:22

229. MANASSEH

He was a WICKED man – 2 Chron. 33:2

He was an IDOLATROUS man – 2 Chron. 33:3

He was a PRIVILEGED man – 2 Chron. 33:10

He was a SELF-WILLED man – 2 Chron. 33:10

He was an AFFLICTED man – 2 Chron. 33:12

He was a HUMBLE man – 2 Chron. 33:12

He was a PRAYING man – 2 Chron. 33:13

He was a SAVED man – 2 Chron. 33:13

230. MARKS OF A TRUE SERVANT

His FAITH – Acts 6:5

His POWER – Acts 6:8

His WISDOM – Acts 6:10

His ENERGY – Acts 6:10

His STEDFASTNESS – Acts 7:55

His COUNTENANCE – Acts 6:15

His TENDERNESS – Acts 7:60

His HOPE – Acts 7:59

231. MERCY

The AUTHOR – 1 Pet. 1:3

The GROUND – Rom. 3:25

The SUBJECTS – Luke 17:13

The CHARACTER – Psa. 103:4

The MEASURE – Psa. 103:8

The EXTENT – Psa. 103:11

The DURATION – Psa. 103:17

232. THE MEEK

Shall be satisfied – Psa. 22:26

Shall be guided – Psa. 25:9

Shall be taught – Psa. 25:9

Shall have inheritance – Psa. 37:11

Shall be saved – Psa. 76:9

Shall be lifted up – Psa. 147:6

Shall be beautified – Psa. 149:4

233. MORE EXCELLENT
Christ has a more excellent name than angels – Heb. 1:4

Faith is a more excellent sacrifice than works – Heb. 2:4

Christ's ministry for no is more excellent than Old Testament priests – Heb. 8:6

234. THE MORNING
PRAYER in the morning – Psa. 5:3

HELP in the morning – Psa. 46:5

JOY in the morning – Psa. 30:5

MERCIES in the morning – Lam. 3:23

SACRIFICES in the morning Amo 4:4

STRENGTH in the morning – Isa. 33:2

LOVING-KINDNESS in the morning – Psa. 143:8

235. "MY" IN JOHN'S GOSPEL
My PEACE – John 14:27

My WORDS – John 15:7

My LOVE – John 15:9

My DISCIPLES – John 15:8

My FRIENDS – John 15:14

My COMMANDMENT – John 15:12

My JOY – John 17:13

My GLORY – John 17:24

236. NEHEMIAH HAD SIX FORMS OF OPPOSITION IN HIS WORK

The GRIEF of the enemy – Neh. 2:10

The LAUGHTER of the enemy – Neh. 2:19

The WRATH of the enemy – Neh. 4:1

The MOCKING of the enemy – Neh. 4:1

The CONFLICT of the enemy – Neh. 4:8

The SUBTLETY of the enemy – Neh. 6:2-3

237. NEVER

Never THIRST – John 4:14

Never HUNGER – John 6:35

Never DIE – John 11:26

Never PERISH – John 10:28

Never LEAVE – Heb. 13:5

Never FALL – 2 Pet. 1:10

Never BE MOVED – Psa. 15:5

238. NICODEMUS

INQUIRING – John 3:2

CONFESSING – John 7:50

WORKING – John 19:39

239. NINE STEPS IN PETER'S LIFE

His CALL – Luke 5:10

His OBEDIENCE – Luke 5:11

His UNBELIEF – Matt. 14:28

Using CARNAL Weapons – Luke 22:50

DEPARTURE from the Lord – Luke 22:54

His ASSOCIATION – Luke 22:55

His DENIAL of his Lord – Luke 22:57

His REPENTANCE – Luke 22:61-62

His SUCCESS – Acts 2:37, 41

240. "NO MORE"
No more CONSCIENCE of sin – Heb. 10:2

No more REMEMBRANCE of sin – Heb. 10:17

No more OFFERING for sin – Heb. 10:18

No more SACRIFICE for sin – Heb. 10:26

241. ONE ANOTHER
LOVE one another – John 13:34

CARE for one another – 1 Cor. 12:25

EXHORT one another – Heb. 3:13

PRAY for one another – James 5:16

Be KIND to one another – Eph. 4:32

FORGIVE one another – Eph. 4:32

SUBMIT one to another – Eph. 5:21

242. OPERATIONS OF THE HOLY SPIRIT
He CONVICTS of sin – John 16:8

He QUICKENS into life – John 3:5-8

He SANCTIFIES – 2 Thess. 2:13

He GUIDES – John 16:13

He COMFORTS – John 14:26

He INTERCEDES – Rom. 8:26

He WITNESSES to our relationship – Rom. 8:16

He INDWELLS each believer – John 14:17

He SEALS us – Eph. 1:13

He BAPTIZES into one body – 1 Cor. 12:13

243. OUR CROWNING BLESSING
Blessed with all spiritual blessings in Christ – Eph. 1:3

In whom we are accepted – Eph. 1:6

In whom we have redemption – Eph 1:7

In whom we have forgiveness – Col. 1:14

Through whom we have peace with God – Rom. 5:1

Through whom we have eternal life – 1 Tim. 6:12

Through whom we have . . . access unto the Father – Eph. 2:18

By whom we are called unto eternal glory – 1 Pet. 5:10

Our crowning joy will be when we shall see Him as He is – 1 John 3:2

244. OUR FEET
THE FEET BY NATURE

Stumbling – Psalm 73:2

Running to evil – Pro. 1:16

Running to mischief – Pro. 6:18

On the dark mountains – Jer. 13:16

Sunk in the mire – Jer. 38:22

Swift to shed blood – Rom. 3:15

Slip in due time – Deu. 32:35

THE FEET BY GRACE

Washed – John 13:10

Kept – 1 Sam. 2:9

Set upon a rock – Psalm 40:2

Not to be moved – Psalm 66:9

Shod with the Gospel – Eph. 6:15

Bringing the Gospel – Rom. 10:15

Bruising Satan – Rom. 16:20

245. OUR GOD

God for us – Rom. 8:31

God in us – Phil. 2:13

God with us – Gen. 28:15

God before us – Exo. 13:21

God above us – Exo. 14:19

God underneath us – Psa. 18:16

God round us – Deu. 33.27

God over us – Psa. 125:2

246. OUR GREAT DELIVERER (2 COR 1:10)

YESTERDAY — Those who have believed on the Lord Jesus Christ can say – "who *delivered us* from so great a death" (NKJV)

TODAY — And trusting Him day by day can add, "and *does deliver us*"

FOREVER.—Then looking forward to the future can say again, "in whom we trust that He *will still deliver* us."

In the past He has *delivered*, in the present He *does deliver*, in the future He *will still deliver*. What a wonderful deliverance!

247. OUR HEARTS
THE HEART BY NATURE

Only evil continually – Gen. 6:5

Gathers iniquity – Psalm 41:6

Of little worth – Pro. 10:20

Perverse – Pro. 12:8

Proud – Pro. 16:5

Deceived – Isa. 44:20

Deceitful – Jer. 17:9

THE HEART BY GRACE

Broken – Psalm 51:17

Clean – Psalm 51:10

New – Eze. 36:26

Having the love of God -Rom. 5:5

Having the peace of God – Col. 3:15

Singing with grace – Col. 3:16

Christ indwelling – Eph. 3:17

248. OUR HOPE
The Coming of the Lord is-

A saving hope – Rom. 8:24

A good hope – 2 Thess. 2:16

A blessed hope – Titus 2:13

A joyful hope – Heb. 3:6

A living hope – 1 Pet. 1:3

A purifying hope – 1 John 3:3

A hope of righteousness – Gal. 5:5

249. OUR LIPS
THE LIPS BY NATURE

Unclean – Isa. 6:5

Uncircumcised – Exo. 6:12

Flattering – Psalm 12:2-3

Lying – Pro. 12:19

Deceitful – Pro. 26:24

Contentious – Prov 18.6

Holding the poison of asps – Rom. 3:13

THE LIPS BY GRACE

Opened – Psalm 51:15

Sinning not – Job 2:10

Joyful – Psalm 63:5

Praising – Psalm 119:171

Keeping knowledge – Pro. 5:2

Dispersing knowledge – Pro. 15:7

Giving thanks – Heb. 13:15

250. OUR MOUTHS
THE MOUTH BY NATURE

Full of cursing and deceit – Psalm 10:7

Speaking proudly – Psalm 17:10

Given to evil – Psalm 1:19

Speaking vanity – Psalm 144:8

Covered with violence – Pro. 10:6

Pouring out foolishness – Pro. 15:2

Ends in destruction – Pro. 18:7

THE MOUTH BY GRACE

Crying unto the Lord – Psalm 66:17

Filled with His praise – Psalm 71:8

Showing his righteousness – Psalm 71:15

Filled with laughter – Psalm 126:2

A well of life – Pro. 10:2

Satisfied – Pro. 18:20

Confessing the Lord Jesus – Rom. 10:9

251. OUR PRIVILEGES AS GOD'S PEOPLE

Our PERFECTION – Col. 2:10

Our PORTION – Eph. 1:3

Our POSITION – Eph. 1:3

Our PROCLAMATION – 2 Tim. 4:2

Our PROGRESS – Psa. 63:8

Our PROTECTION – Psa. 31:20

Our PROSPERITY – Josh. 1:8

Our PROSPECT – John 14:3

252. OUR RESURRECTION BODY
Like CHRIST'S – Phil. 3:21

ETERNAL – 2 Cor. 5:1

REDEEMED – Rom. 8:23

INCORRUPTIBLE – 1 Cor. 15:42

GLORIOUS – 1 Cor. 15:43

POWERFUL – 1 Cor. 15:43

SPIRITUAL – 1 Cor. 15:44

253. OUR UNION WITH CHRIST
RECEIVE Him – Col. 2:6

WALK in Him – Col. 2:6

ROOTED in Him – Col. 2:7

COMPLETE in Him – Col. 2:10

DIED with Him – Col. 2:20

BURIED with Him – Col. 2:12

RAISED with Him – Col. 3:1

APPEARING with Him – Col. 3:4

254. PARTAKERS
DIVINE NATURE – 2 Pet. 1:4

SUFFERINGS – 1 Pet. 4:13

CHASTISEMENT – Heb. 12:8

CALLING – Heb. 3:1

INHERITANCE – Col. 1:12

GLORY – 1 Pet. 5:1

HOLINESS – Heb. 12:10

255. THE PATH
STRAIGHT path – Heb. 12:13

NARROW path – Matt. 7:14

PLAIN path – Psa. 27:11

PEACEFUL path – Prov. 3:17

SHINING path – Prov. 4:18

OLD path – Jer. 6:16

FRUITFUL path – Psa. 65:11

256. THE PATIENT AND PHYSICIAN
THE PATIENT —

    His Helplessness – John 5:6

    His Willingness – John 5:7

    His Ignorance – John 5:7

    His Obedience – John 5:9

THE PHYSICIAN —

    He Saw Him – John 5:6

    He Spoke to Him – John 5:6

    He Healed Him – John 5:9

    He Commanded Him – John 5:8

257. PAUL SUFFERED WHAT SAUL INFLICTED
Saul at the stoning of Stephen – Acts 7:58

Paul stoned – 2 Cor. 11:25

Saul persecuting – Gal. 1:13

Paul persecuted – 2 Cor. 11:24

Saul binding – Acts 22:4

Paul bound – Acts 24:27

Saul imprisoning – Acts 8:3

Paul imprisoned – 2 Cor. 11:23

Saul delivering to death – Acts 22:4

Paul in deaths oft – 2 Cor. 11:23

258. PAUL'S ACTION IN ACTS 27
PAUL ADMONISHING – v.9

PAUL EXHORTING – v.22

PAUL CONFESSING – v.23

PAUL CONFIDING – v.25

PAUL COUNSELLING – v.31

PAUL BESEECHING – v.33

PAUL'S THANKSGIVING – v.35

259. PAUL'S COURSE
Paul's PRAYERFULNESS – Acts 21:5

Paul's DILIGENCE – Acts 21:7-8

Paul's COURAGE – Acts 21:13

Paul's WEAKNESS – Acts 21:23-26

Paul's SUFFERING – Acts 21:32

Paul's TESTIMONY – Acts 21:40

260. PAUL'S DESIRE
To KNOW Christ – Phil. 3:10

To WIN Christ – Phil. 3:8

To be CONFORMED to Christ – Phil. 3:10

To MAGNIFY Christ – Phil. 1:20

To be FOUND in Christ – Phil. 3:9

To REJOICE in Christ – Phil. 2:16

To BE WITH Christ – Phil. 1:23

261. PAUL'S FAITHFULNESS TO TIMOTHY
Paul the Prisoner, and Timothy Strengthened – 2 Tim. 1

Paul the Servant, and Timothy Encouraged – 2 Tim. 2

Paul the Witness, and Timothy Warned – 2 Tim. 3

Paul the Martyr, and Timothy Charged – 2 Tim. 4

262. PAUL'S THREEFOLD THANKSGIVING
For the GIFT – 2 Cor. 9:15

For the TRIUMPH – 2 Cor. 2:14

For the VICTORY – 1 Cor. 15:57

263. PAUL'S TWOFOLD EXPERIENCE
LET DOWN by the wall – 2 Cor. 11:33

CAUGHT UP to the third heaven – 2 Cor. 12:2

264. PEACE
NEEDED – John 20:19

MADE – Col. 1:20

GIVEN – John 14:27

POSSESSED – Rom. 5:1

ENJOYED – John 20:19-20

PROCLAIMED – Luke 2:14

RULING – Col. 3:15

265. PEACE AND NO PEACE
Profession – Jer. 6:14

Perplexity – Isa. 38:17

Proposal – Job 22:21

Purchase – Col. 1:20

Preached – Eph 2:17

Possessed – Rom. 5:1

Perdition – Isa. 57. 21

266. PEACE IN TWO ASPECTS
Peace *with* God – Peace of Reconciliation – Rom. 5:1

Peace *of* God – Peace of rest, confidence, and satisfaction – Phil. 4:7

267. PERFECTION
The FATHER – Matt. 5:48

His WORK – Deu. 32:4

His WAY – Psa. 18:30

His WILL – Rom. 12:2

His LOVE – 1 John 4:18

His LAW – Psa. 19:7

His GIFTS – James 1:17

268. PERFECTION OF THE LORD JESUS

In Him was no sin – 1 John 3:5

He knew no sin – 2 Cor. 5:21

He committed no sin – 1 Pet. 2:22

He was without sin – Heb 4:15

And yet He His own self bore our sins in His own body on the tree – 1 Pet. 2:24

269. PICTURE OF A RIGHTEOUS MAN

The WAY of the Righteous – Psa. 1:6

The INHERITANCE of the Righteous – Psa. 37:29

The GLADNESS of the Righteous – Psa. 64:10

The FLOURISHING of the Righteous – Psa. 92:12

The REMEMBRANCE of the Righteous – Psa. 112:6

The THANKSGIVING of the Righteous – Psa. 140:13

The SAFETY of the Righteous – Prov. 18:10

The RECOMPENSE of the Righteous – Prov. 11:21

270. PICTURE OF MAN IN THE BOOK OF JOB

His RUIN – Job 33:24

His RANSOM – Job 33:24

His REGENERATION – Job 33:24

His RECONCILIATION – Job 34:26

His REST – Job 33:26

His RIGHTEOUSNESS – Job 33:26

271. PILGRIM'S PROGRESS IN PSALM 63

My soul thirsts for You – v.1

My soul shall be satisfied – v.5

My soul follows after You – v.8

272. THE PLACE

A LARGE place – Psa. 18:19

A WEALTHY place – Psa. 66:12

A SECRET place – Psa. 91:1

A HIDING place – Isa. 32:2

A SURE place – Isa. 22:23

The BEST place – John 14:2

273. POWER OF THE TRINITY

The Power of God – 2 Cor. 6:7

The Power of the Lord – Col. 1:11; Eph. 6:10

The Power of the Spirit – Luke 4:14; Eph. 3:16; Rom. 15:13

274. POWER PRINCIPLES

Great power – Acts 4:33

Mighty power – Eph. 1:19

Excellent power – 2 Cor. 4:7

Exceeding great power – Eph. 1:19

Divine power – 2 Pet. 1:3

Eternal power – Rom. 1:20

Glorious power – Col. 1:11

275. PRAYER
WHERE TO PRAY: —

> In private – Matt. 6:6
>
> In public – Acts 1:14

HOW TO PRAY: —

> In the Holy Spirit – Jude v.20
>
> In faith – James 1:6
>
> With the understanding – 1 Cor. 14:15

WHAT WE SHOULD PRAY FOR: —

> All saints – Eph. 6:18
>
> All men – 1 Tim. 2:1
>
> All things – Phil. 4:6

WHEN GOD ANSWERS PRAYER: —

> Sometimes at once – Isa. 65:24
>
> Sometimes after delay – Luke 18:7
>
> Sometimes differently from what we expect – 2 Cor. 12:8-9

WHAT HINDERS OUR PRAYERS: —

> Asking amiss – James 4:3
>
> Unbelief – James 1:6-7
>
> Iniquity in the heart – Psa. 66:18

276. PRAYER (2)
WHY PRAY?

The prayer of a righteous man avails much – James 5:16

Lest we enter into temptation – Mat.t 26:41

We are commanded to do so – Luke 18:1

HOW TO PRAY

In the Spirit – Eph. 6:18

In the Holy Spirit – Jude v.20

Laboring fervently – Col. 4:12

With understanding – 1 Cor. 14:14-15

With holy hands-without wrath or doubting – 1 Tim. 2:8

Ask in faith, without wavering – James 1:6

WHEN TO PRAY

In times of danger - men filled with madness – Luke 6:12

Evening, morning, and at noon-day – Psa. 55:17

Pray without ceasing – 1 Thess. 5:17

In affliction – James 5:13

In sickness – James 5:14

When we have transgressed one against another – James 5:16

WHAT TO PRAY FOR

For laborers to be sent forth into the harvest – Matt. 9:37-38

All men, kings all in authority – 1 Tim. 2:1-2

Filled with the knowledge of the Lord's will – Col. 1:9-11

For those who despitefully use you – Matt. 5:44

In everything – Phil. 4:6

Lord, teach us how to pray Luke 11:1

277. PRECIOUS THINGS
REDEMPTION – Psa. 49:8

NAME – 1 Sam. 18:30

WORD of the Lord – 1 Sam. 3:1

LOVINGKINDNESS – Psa. 36:7

WISDOM – Prov. 3:13-15

THOUGHTS – Psa. 139:17

FRUITS – Deu. 33:14

278. THE PRE-EMINENT ONE
in Hebrews 1

Future Ruler – "Heir of all things"

Past Creator – "He made the worlds"

Eternal Son – "Express Image of His person"

Present Upholder – "Upholding all things"

Sin Purger – "Purged our sins"

Enthroned Prince – "Sat down on throne"

Coming King – "He brings again"

279. PRIVILEGES AND RESPONSIBILITIES
REDEEMING — God – Eph. 1:7

REDEEMING — Man – Eph. 5:16

RECEIVING – Col. 2:6

RECONCILING — God's side – 2 Cor. 5:19

RECONCILING — Man's side – Matt. 5:24

RECKONING – Rom. 6:11

RECOVERING – 2 Tim. 2:26

REFRAINING – 1 Pet. 3:10

REJOICING — Extent – Phil. 4:10

REJOICING — Duration – Phil. 4:4

REIGNING – Rev. 22:5

280. PROOFS OF CHRIST'S LOVE TO THE CHURCH

He GAVE Himself for it – Eph. 5:25

He UNITES it to Himself – Eph. 5:31-32

He SANCTIFIES it – Eph. 5:26

He CLEANSES it – Eph. 5:26

He NOURISHES it – Eph. 5:29

He CHERISHES it – Eph. 5:29

He will PRESENT it – Eph. 5:27

281. PSALM 4

SEPARATION — Set apart – v.3

CONFIDENCE — The Lord will hear – v.3

COMMAND — Sin not – v.4

WORSHIP — Offer the sacrifice – v.5

EXHORTATION — Trust in the Lord – v.5

PRAYER — Lift up – v.6

JOY — Gladness in my heart – v.7

REST — Lay me down – v.8

SECURITY — Dwell in safety – v.8

282. PSALM 16:11

The PATH

The PRESENCE

The PROSPECT

283. PSALM 23 (version 1)

POSSESSION – My Shepherd

PROVISION – Not want

POSITION – Lie down

PASTURES – Green grass

PROGRESS – Walk

PLACE – Valley

PRESENCE – With Me

PROTECTION – Rod and Staff

PREPARATION – Prepares, etc.

PLENTY – Running over

PURSUING – Shall Pursue

PROSPECT – House of the Lord for ever

284. PSALM 23 (version 2)

WITH me – The Lord

BENEATH me – Green pastures

BESIDE me – Still waters

BEFORE me – A table

AROUND me – Mine enemies

AFTER me – Goodness and Mercy

BEYOND me – House of the Lord

285. PSALM 23 (version 3)
Perfect SATISFACTION – "Shall not want."

Perfect REST – "Lying down."

Perfect PEACE – "Waters of quietness."

Perfect WALK – "Paths of righteousness."

Perfect CONFIDENCE – "Will fear no evil."

Perfect POWER – "Anoint my head."

Perfect JOY – "My cup runneth over."

286. PSALM 32
BLESSING, when sin is covered – v.1

FORGIVENESS, when sin is confessed – v.5

PRESERVATION in time of trouble – v.7

SINGING in time of deliverance – v.7

INSTRUCTION in time of ignorance – v.8

GUIDANCE in time of uncertainty – v.8

REJOICING in time of uprightness – v.11

287. PSALM 40
My State – v.2

My Salvation – v.2

My Standing – v.2

My Safety – v.2

My Song – v.3

My Service – v.3

288. PSALM 59:16

WHAT I do "I will sing"

HOW I do it "sing aloud"

WHEN I do it "in the morning"

WHY I do it "You have been my defense"

289. PSALM 63

CONFIDENCE "My God"

DESIRE "My soul thirsts"

JOY "My lips shall praise"

SATISFACTION "My soul shall be satisfied"

MEDITATION "Meditate on You"

PROGRESS "My soul follows hard"

SAFETY "Your right hand upholds me"

290. PSALM 84

Blessed is the man that DWELLS – v.4

Blessed is the man that is STRONG – v.5

Blessed is the man that TRUSTS – v.12

291. PSALM 86

The soul's need — "For I am poor" – v.1

Covenant relationship — "For I am holy" – v.2

Constant communion — "For I cry daily" – v.3

Singleness of desire — "For unto Thee" – v.4

God's character — "For Thou art good" – v.5

Full assurance — "For Thou wilt answer" – v.7

God's power — "For Thou art great" – v.10

Past favors — "For Thy mercy is great" – v.13

292. PSALM 136
God as my CREATOR – vv.5-9

God as my DELIVERER – v.11

God as my GUIDE – v.16

God as my GIVER – v.21

God as my REMEMBRANCER – v.23

God as my REDEEMER – v.24

God as my PROVIDER – v.25

293. THE PSALMIST'S DETERMINATION
I will EXTOL THEE – Psa. 145:1

I will BLESS Thy Name – Psa. 145:1

I will PRAISE Thy Name – Psa. 145:2

I will SPEAK of the Honor of Thy Majesty – Psa. 145:5

I will DECLARE Thy Greatness – Psa. 145:6

294. THE PURSUIT OF JOY
Fruit of Joy – Gal. 5:22

Great joy – Luke 2:10

Exceeding joy – 1 Pet. 4:13

Exceeding great joy – Matt. 2:10

Abundance of joy – 2 Cor. 8:2

Fulness of joy – John 15:11

Unspeakable joy – 1 Pet. 1:8

295. QUANTITIES OF FRUIT
Some fruit – Rom. 1:13

More fruit – John 15:2

Much fruit – John 15:8

Abounding fruit – Phil. 4:17

Hundred-fold fruit – Luke 8:8

296. QUALITY OF FRUIT
Good fruit – Matt. 7:17

Precious fruit – James 5:7

Sweet fruit – Song 2:3

Permanent fruit – John 15:16

Pleasant fruit – Song 4:16

297. THE QUEEN OF SHEBA
She HEARD — The Ear – 1 Kings 10:1

She CAME — The Feet – 1 Kings 10:1

She COMMUNED — The Heart – 1 Kings 10:2

She LEARNED — The Mind – 1 Kings 10:3

She BEHELD — The Eyes – 1 Kings 10:4, 5

She EXCLAIMED — The Tongue – 1 Kings 10:8, 9

She GAVE — The Hands – 1 Kings 10:10

298. RAHAB
Her CONDITION – Josh. 2:1

Her FAITH – Josh. 2:9

Her EARNESTNESS – Josh. 2:12, 14

Her REQUEST – Josh. 2:12

Her DELIVERANCE – Josh. 6:23

Her SAFETY – Josh. 6:25

299. READY
The believer should be "ready" -

To give an answer of the hope – 1 Pet. 3:15

To preach the gospel – Rom. 1:15

To distribute – 1 Tim. 6:18

To every good work – Titus 3:1

To be bound – Acts 21:13

To be offered – 2 Tim. 4:6

To meet the Lord – Luke 12:40

300. REALITIES
The living GOD – Psa. 84:2

A living SOUL – Gen. 2:7

The living WORD – Heb. 4:12

The living BREAD – John 6:51

The living WATER – John 4:10

The living WAY – Heb. 10:20

The living SACRIFICE – Rom. 12:1

The living HOPE – 1 Pet. 1:3

301. REASONS FOR NOT FEARING
He REDEEMS me – Isa. 43:1

He PROTECTS me – Gen. 15:1

He STRENGTHENS me – Isa. 35:4

He is WITH me – Isa. 41:10

He HELPS me – Isa. 41:13

He CARES for me – Matt. 10:31

He has a KINGDOM for me – Luke 12:32

302. RECONCILIATION IN 2 Cor. 5:18-20

The NEED of reconciliation

The GROUND of reconciliation

The MINISTRY of reconciliation

The RESULT of reconciliation

303. REDEMPTION

I. What I am redeemed with —

    By BLOOD – 1 Pet. 1:19

    By POWER – Neh. 1:10

II. What I am redeemed from —

    BONDAGE – Exo. 6:6

    ENEMY – Psa. 106:10

    INIQUITY – Tit. 2:14

    CURSE OF THE LAW – Gal. 3:13

III. What the Lord has redeemed —

    The SOUL – Psa. 49:8

    The BODY – Rom. 8:23

    The LIFE – Psa. 103:4

IV. The Beauty of the Redemption —

It is PLENTEOUS – Psa. 130:7

It is PRECIOUS – Psa. 49:8

It is ETERNAL – Heb. 9:12

304. REJOICING

The OBJECT of our rejoicing – Phil. 3:1

The CHARACTER of it – Phil. 1:26

The DURATION of it – Phil. 4:4

The PLACE of rejoicing – Psa. 63:7

The CAUSE of our rejoicing —

    His SALVATION – Psa. 20:5

    His NAME – Psa. 89:16

    His GOODNESS – 2 Chron. 6:411

    His TRUTH – 1 Cor. 13:6

    The HOPE – Rom. 5:2

    Our NAMES, written in heaven – Luke 10:20

305. REPENTANCE

The NATURE of – Matt. 21:9

The SOURCE of – 2 Tim. 2:25

The NECESSITY for – Acts 8:22

The RESULTS of – Luke 15:7; – Luke 17:3

By WHOM commanded – Acts 17:30

In WHOSE name – Luke 24:47

306. REPRESENTATIVE PERSONS IN PSALM 23

The SHEPHERD to be obeyed – v.1

The TRAVELLER to be rested – v.2

The WANDERER to be restored – v.3

The TIMID to be comforted – v.4

The WARRIOR to be feasted – v.5

The PRIEST to be anointed – v.5

The PILGRIM to be housed – v.6

307. RESULT OF A PRAYER MEETING

They possessed great boldness – Acts 4:31

They were united in heart – Acts 4:32

They consecrated all they had – Acts 4:32

They displayed great simplicity – Acts 4:32

They witnessed with great power – Acts 4:33

They showed great grace – Acts 4:33

They had care for one another – Acts 4:34

They were in complete subjection – Acts 4:35

308. RESULT OF PETER'S PREACHING ON THE DAY OF PENTECOST

The people were AMAZED – Acts 2:12

They MOCKED – Acts 2:13

They HEARD – Acts 2:37

They were CONVICTED – Acts 2:37

They INQUIRED – Acts 2:37

They were CONVERTED – Acts 2:41

They were STEDFAST – Acts 2:42

They were UNITED – Acts 2:44

They were SELF-DENYING – Acts 2:45

They were PRAISING God – Acts 2:47

309. RESULTS OF OVERCOMING
EAT of the tree of life – Rev. 2:7

DELIVERANCE from the second death – Rev. 2:11

FEAST on the hidden manna – Rev. 2:17

POWER over the nations – Rev. 2:26

CLOTHED in white raiment – Rev. 3:5

PILLAR in God's temple – Rev. 3:12

SEATED on His throne – Rev. 3:21

INHERIT all things – Rev. 21:7

310. REVELATION 21:6
The GIVER – God

To WHOM He gives – The thirsty

WHAT He gives – The water of life

HOW HE gives – Freely

311. THE REWARD
SURE reward – Prov. 11:18

GREAT reward – Luke 6:35

FULL reward – 2 John 1:8

OPEN reward – Matt. 6:6

DEGREES of reward – 2 Tim. 4:14

DANGER of losing reward – 2 John 1:8

The TIME of the reward – Rev. 22:12

312. THE RICH FARMER
A PROSPEROUS man – Luke 12:16

An UNGODLY man – Luke 12:17

An EARTHLY-MINDED man – Luke 12:18

A PRESUMPTUOUS man – Luke 12:19

A FOOLISH man – Luke 12:20

A LOST man – Luke 12:20

313. THE ROCK
On the Rock for my FOUNDATION – Matt. 7:24

In the Rock for my SAFETY – Song 2:14

Under the Rock for my REST – Isa. 32:2

Out of the Rock my SUPPLY: —

    Water — refreshment – Deu. 8:15

    Honey — satisfaction – Psa. 81:16

    Oil — power – Deu. 32:13

    Fire — consuming – Judges 6:12

314. THE ROCK OF
SALVATION – Psa. 89:26

REFUGE – Psa. 94:22

STRENGTH – Isa. 17:10

REST – Isa. 32:2

REFRESHMENT – Neh. 9:15

DEFENCE – Isa. 33:16

SATISFACTION – Psa. 81:16

REJOICING – Isa. 42:11

315. ROMANS 3:23-25
A solemn FACT – "All have sinned"

A terrible FAILURE – "Come short"

A blessed TRUTH – Man justified

A glorious RESULT – Sins forgiven

316. ROMANS 3:27-29
BOASTING EXCLUDED

JUSTIFICATION CONCLUDED

GENTILES INCLUDED

317. RUTH
Ruth — CLEAVING – Ruth 1

Ruth — In the field of Boaz – Ruth 2

Ruth — At the feet of Boaz – Ruth 3

Ruth — United to Boaz – Ruth 4

318. RUTH'S SERVICE
She was ACTIVE in her service – Ruth 2:2

She STAYED where she was placed – Ruth 2:8, 23

She SHOWED great humility – Ruth 2:10

She LEFT ALL for Boaz – Ruth 2:11

She was REWARDED for her work – Ruth 2:12

She TRUSTED in the Lord – Ruth 2:12

She was REFRESHED during her service – Ruth 2:14

She was SATISFIED with what she had – Ruth 2:18

319. THE SAINTS ARE TO BE
RAISED – 1 Cor. 15:52

CHANGED – Phil. 3:21

MANIFESTED – 2 Cor. 5:10

PRESENTED – Eph. 5:27

And to APPEAR – Col. 3:4

320. THE SAINT'S POSITION
In His HAND — For safety – Deu. 33:3

At His FEET — For learning – Deu. 33:3

At His SIDE — For fellowship – Deu. 33:12

Between His SHOULDERS — For power – Deu. 33:12

In His ARMS — For rest – Deu. 33:27

321. SALVATION
Its AUTHOR – Jonah 2:9

The WAY of it – Acts 16:17

The KNOWLEDGE of it – Luke 1:77

The JOY of it – Psa. 51:12

The SEASON of it – 2 Cor. 6:2

The DURATION of it – Heb. 5:9

322. SALVATION DESCRIBED
A COMMON salvation – Jude v.3

A PRESENT salvation – 2 Cor. 6:2

A GREAT salvation – Heb. 2:3

An ETERNAL salvation – Heb. 5:9

An ACCOMPLISHED salvation – John 19:30

A PROGRESSIVE salvation – Phil. 2:12

A PROSPECTIVE salvation – Rom. 13:11

323. SALVATION IS
Salvation is free – Eph. 2:8

Salvation is seen – Luke 2:29-30

Salvation is everlasting – John 3:16

Salvation is now – 2 Cor. 6:2

324. SAMUEL
PROGRESSIVE one — "grew" – 1 Sam. 3:19

PRIVILEGED one — Lord with him – 1 Sam. 3:19

POWERFUL one — None of his words, etc. – 1 Sam. 3:19

PROSPEROUS one — A prophet of the Lord – 1 Sam. 3:20

325. SAUL'S CONVERSION
What he DID – Acts 9:4

What he HEARD – Acts 9:4

What he SAW – Acts 9:3

What he SAID – Acts 9:5

What he BECAME – Acts 9:15

326. THE SAVIOR
Saved – John 3:17

Accepted – Eph. 1:6

Inheritance – 1 Pet. 1:4

Obtain – 2 Tim. 2:10

Unblamable – Col. 1:22

Rejoice – Phil. 3:1

327. SCENE IN THE TEMPLE
Power of SILENCE – John 8:6

Power of CONSCIENCE – John 8:9

Power of LOVE – John 8:11

328. THE SCOFFERS
Their WALK – 2 Pet. 3:3

Their QUESTION – 2 Pet. 3:4

Their IGNORANCE – 2 Pet. 3:5

329. THE SERVANT
GENERAL servant – 1 Cor. 9:19

WISE servant – Matt. 24:45

WATCHFUL servant – Luke 12:37

DEPENDENT servant – Dan. 9:17

HAPPY servant – 2 Chron. 9:7

FAITHFUL servant – Matt. 25:21

REWARDED servant – Rev. 22:12

330. THE SERVANT IS TO —

WALK – 1 Thess. 4:12

WATCH – 1 Thess. 5:6

WAIT – 1 Thess. 1:10

WITNESS – 1 Thess. 1:7

WARN – 1 Thess. 5:14

WORK – 1 Thess. 1:3

331. SERVICE

CHOSEN for service – Matt. 20:16

PREPARED for service – 2 Tim. 2:21

FREE for service – Ezra 1:3

UNITED for service – Ezra 3:1

SUCCESSFUL in service – Ezra 3:10-11

JOYFUL in service – Psa. 126:6

REWARDED for service – Matt. 25:23

332. SEVEN ASPECTS OF LOVE

Infinite – John 15:9

Everlasting – Jer. 31:3

Perfect – Gal. 2:20

Unchanging – John 13:1

Inseparable – Rom. 8:35

Constraining – 2 Cor. 5:14

Commended – Rom. 5:8

333. SEVEN ASPECTS OF PREACHING
Preaching the WORD – Acts 8:4

Preaching CHRIST – Acts 8:5

Preaching the KINGDOM – Acts 8:12

Preaching the WORD of the Lord – Acts 8:25

Preaching the GOSPEL – Acts 8:25

Preaching JESUS – Acts 8:35

Preaching EVERYWHERE – Acts 8:40

334. SEVEN ASPECTS OF SALVATION
HORN of Salvation — Power – Luke 1:69

ROCK of Salvation — Stability – Psa. 95:1

TOWER of Salvation — Security – 2 Sam. 22:51

HELMET of Salvation — Preservation – 1 Thess. 5:8

CUP of Salvation — Joy – Psa. 116:13

WELLS of Salvation — Refreshment – Isa. 12:3

GARMENTS of Salvation — Victory – Isa. 61:10

335. SEVEN ASPECTS OF THE GOSPEL
FELLOWSHIP in the Gospel – Phil. 1:5

PROGRESS in the Gospel – Phil. 1:12

DEFENDING the Gospel – Phil. 1:17

LIVING in the Gospel – Phil. 1:27

FAITH in the Gospel – Phil. 1:27

SERVING in the Gospel – Phil. 2:22

LABORING in the Gospel – Phil. 4:3

336. SEVEN BLESSINGS IN PHILIPPIANS 4

Pardon – verse 3 – Whose names are in the Book of Life

Praise – verse 4 – Rejoice in the Lord always

Prospect – verse 5 – The Lord is at hand

Peace – verse 7 – The peace of God

Presence – verse 9 – The God of peace with us

Power – verse 13 – I can do all things through Christ

Provision – verse 19 – My God shall supply all your need

337. SEVEN BLESSINGS IN ROMANS 5

Peace – verse 1 – We have peace with God

Place – verse 2 – Access by faith...wherein we stand

Prospect – verse 2 – Rejoice in hope of the glory of God

Power – verse 5 – Love of God shed abroad...Holy Spirit

Priest – verse 10 – We shall be saved by His life

Portion – verse 11 – We boast in God

Power – verse 11 – Through our lord Jesus Christ

338. SEVEN CHARACTERISTICS OF PHARAOH

IGNORANT man – Exo. 5:2

DISOBEDIENT man – Exo. 5:2

UNBELIEVING man – Exo. 5:9

FOOLISH man – Exo. 8:10

HARDENED man – Exo. 8:15

PRIVILEGED man – Exo. 9:1

LOST man – Exo. 14:26-28

339. SEVEN CHARACTERISTICS OF SAINTS

The SON — Strength – 2 Tim. 2:1

The SOLDIER — Fighting – 2 Tim. 2:3

The HUSBANDMAN — Laboring – 2 Tim. 2:6

The WRESTLER — Conquering – 2 Tim. 2:5

The WORKMAN — Teaching – 2 Tim. 2:15

The VESSELS — Separation – 2 Tim. 2:21

The SERVANT — Gentleness – 2 Tim. 2:24

340. SEVEN CHARACTERISTICS OF SAINTS IN THE PSALMS

HAPPY Saints – Psa. 30:4

LOVING Saints – Psa. 31:23

FEARING Saints – Psa. 34:9

GATHERED Saints – Psa. 50:5

PRESERVED Saints – Psa. 97:10

PRECIOUS Saints – Psa. 116:151

WITNESSING Saints – Psa. 145:10-12

341. SEVEN CHARACTERISTICS OF THE PEOPLE OF GOD

DISCIPLES in the same *school* – One *Master* – Acts 20:7

CHILDREN in the same *family* – One *Father* – John 11:52

SHEEP in the same *flock* – One *Shepherd* – John 10:16

SAINTS in the same *covenant* – One *Rank* – Rom. 1:7

STONES in the same *house* – One *Foundation* – 1 Pet. 2:5

MEMBERS – in the same *body* – One *Head* – Rom. 12:5

THE BRIDE – in the same *glory* – One *Bridegroom* – Rev. 21:2,9

All believers are alike disciples, though some have not made the same progress as others.

All are alike children, sharing the same life, though some of them are mere babes, others young men or fathers in growth.

All are alike sheep, though some follow the Shepherd more closely, listening to His voice.

All are alike saints by calling, though some are more practically holy in their walk and conversation than others.

All are alike living stones upon the one foundation, though some are more prominent in the building than others.

All are alike members of the body, though some have a more honorable place and office than others.

All will be together in the same glory, though some will suffer loss through unfaithfulness when in the body.

342. SEVEN CHARACTERISTICS OF THE SHEEP
They are SAVED by Him – John 10:9

They have LIBERTY from Him – John 10:9

They are CALLED by Him – John 10:3

They are SECURED in Him – John 10:28

They are FED by Him – John 10:9

They are OBEDIENT to Him – John 10:4

They have KNOWLEDGE of Him – John 10:14

343. SEVEN CLASSES IN JOHN 6
The CURIOUS – John 6:2

The ADMIRING – John 6:14

The GREEDY – John 6:26

The SCEPTICAL – John 6:36

The MURMURING – John 6:41

The SCOFFING – John 6:52

The BACKSLIDING – John 6:66

344. SEVEN CLASSES IN PHILIPPIANS
SONS – Phil. 2:15

SAINTS – Phil. 1:1

SERVANTS – Phil. 1:1

BISHOPS – Phil. 1:1

BRETHREN – Phil. 3:17

FELLOW-SOLDIER – Phil. 2:25

FELLOW-LABORER – Phil. 4:3

345. SEVEN CLASSES IN THE DISCIPLES' PRAYER
"Our Father" — The children – Matt. 6:9

"Hallowed be Thy name" — Worshippers – Matt. 6:9

"Thy Kingdom come" — The subjects – Matt. 6:10

"Thy will be done" — The servants – Matt. 6:10

"Give us this day" — The suppliants – Matt. 6:11

"Forgive us our debts" — The confessors – Matt. 6:12

"Deliver us from evil" — The dependents – Matt. 6:13

346. SEVEN CLASSES OF CHILDREN
Children of WRATH – Eph. 2:3

Children of DISOBEDIENCE – Eph. 2:2

Children of UNBELIEF – Eph. 5:6

Children of ADOPTION – Eph. 1:5

Children of LIGHT – Eph. 5:8

Children LOVED – Eph. 5:1, 2

Children COMMANDED – Eph. 6:1

347. SEVEN "DAILY" THINGS
Daily FEEDING – Matt. 6:11

Daily CROSS-BEARING – Luke 9:23

Daily WORKING – Acts 5:42

Daily SEARCHING – Acts 17:11

Daily DYING – 1 Cor. 15:31

Daily EXHORTING – Heb. 3:13

Daily WATCHING – Prov. 8:34

348. SEVEN EVERLASTING THINGS IN ISAIAH
SALVATION – Isa. 45:17

LIGHT – Isa. 60:19

JOY – Isa. 35:10

STRENGTH – Isa. 26:4

KINDNESS – Isa. 54:8

COVENANT – Isa. 55:3

JUDGMENT – Isa. 33:14

349. SEVEN GIFTS
The NAME – Neh. 9:7

The LAND – Neh. 9:8

LIGHT – Neh. 9:12

JUDGMENT – Neh. 9:13

BREAD – Neh. 9:15

The SPIRIT – Neh. 9:20

KINGDOMS – Neh. 9:22

350. SEVEN GIFTS IN JOHN
LIFE for salvation – John 10:11

FLESH for sustenance – John 6:51

PEACE for enjoyment – John 14:27

The SPIRIT our Comforter – John 14:16

WORD for edification – John 17:8

EXAMPLE for imitation – John 13:15

GLORY our goal – John 17:22

351. SEVEN GOOD THINGS
Good CONSCIENCE – 1 Pet. 3:16

Good WORD – Heb. 6:5

Good WORKS – Eph. 2:10

Good COURAGE – Psa. 27:14

Good FRUIT – Matt. 7:17

Good TIDINGS – 1 Thess. 3:6

Good DAY – Est. 9:19

352. SEVEN MANIFOLD THINGS
Man's manifold transgressions – Amos 5:12

God's manifold works – Psa. 104:24

God's manifold wisdom – Eph. 3:10

God's manifold mercies – Neh. 9:27

God's manifold grace – 1 Pet. 4:10

Man's manifold temptations – 1 Pet. 1:6

Man's manifold reward – Luke 18:30

353. SEVEN "NOTS" IN JOHN'S GOSPEL
Shall not perish – 3:16

Shall not thirst – 4:14

Shall not be judged – 5:24

Shall never hunger – 6:35

Shall not walk in darkness – 8:12

Shall not be plucked out of His hand – 10:28

Shall never die – 11:26

354. SEVEN POINTS IN JEREMIAH 1
God knowing him "I knew you."

God sanctifying him "I sanctified you."

God ordaining him "I ordained you."

God sending him "I shall send."

God commanding him "I command."

God encouraging him "Be not afraid."

God speaking through him "I have put my words in your mouth."

355. SEVEN POINTS of MAN'S INSIGNIFICANCE
The People are GRASS – Isa. 40:7

The Nations — A DROP in a BUCKE T– Isa. 40:15

The SMALL DUST of the BALANCE – Isa. 40:15

They are NOTHING – Isa. 40:17

They are LESS than NOTHING – Isa. 40:17

They are VANITY – Isa. 40:17

They are GRASSHOPPERS – Isa. 40:22

356. SEVEN STEPS IN CHRIST'S EXALTATION
Philippians 2:9-11

1. God highly exalted Him-Humanity occupying the highest place in the universe.
2. Given Him a Name which is above every name.
3. At the name of Jesus every knee shall bow.
4. Of things in heaven.
5. And things on earth.
6. And things under the earth.
7. And every tongue confess that Jesus is Lord.

357. SEVEN STEPS IN CHRIST'S HUMILIATION
Philippians 2:7-8

1. Made Himself of no reputation.
2. Took upon Him the form of a servant.
3. Made in the likeness of Men.
4. Found in fashion as a man.
5. Humbled Himself.
6. Became obedient unto death.
7. Even the death of the Cross.

358. SEVEN STEPS IN DAVID'S LIFE
IGNORANCE – 2 Sam. 12:5

CONVICTION – 2 Sam. 12:7

CONFESSION – 2 Sam. 12:13

FORGIVENESS – 2 Sam. 12:13

WORSHIP – 2 Sam. 12:20

FEASTING – 2 Sam. 12:20

VICTORY – 2 Sam. 12:29

359. SEVEN STEPS IN ISRAEL'S EXPERIENCE
CONTRITION – Neh. 9:1

SEPARATION – Neh. 9:2

CONFESSION – Neh. 9:2

INSTRUCTION – Neh. 9:3

WORSHIP – Neh. 9:3

PRAYER – Neh. 9:4

PRAISE – Neh. 9:5

360. SEVEN THINGS ABOUT ISRAEL
A SAVED people – Deu. 33:29

A REMARKABLE people – Deu. 33:29

A HAPPY people – Deu. 33:29

A SHELTERED people – Deu. 33:29

A DEFENDED people – Deu. 33:29

A MALIGNED people – Deu. 33:29

A VICTORIOUS people – Deu. 33:29

361. SEVEN THINGS ABOUT THE RICH MAN
His CONDITION — rich – Luke 16:19

His CHARACTER — religious (Jew) – Luke 16:24

His POSITION — in need – Luke 16:23

His PRAYER — "have mercy" – Luke 16:24

His SUFFERING — "I am tormented" – Luke 16:24

His CONSCIENCE — Son, remember – Luke 16:25

His SEPARATION — great gulf fixed – Luke 16:26

362. SEVEN THINGS ACCOMPLISHED
You have LIFTED me up – Psa. 30:1

You have HEALED me – Psa. 30:2

You have BROUGHT up my soul from death – Psa. 30:3

You have KEPT me alive – Psa. 30:3

You have MADE my mountain to stand strong – Psa. 30:7

You have TURNED my mourning into dancing – Psa. 30:11

You have GIRDED me with goodness – Psa. 30:11

363. SEVEN THINGS GOD DOES IN GENESIS 1
He CREATES – Gen. 1:1

He MOVES – Gen. 1:2

He SPEAKS – Gen. 1:3

He OBSERVES – Gen. 1:4

He CALLS – Gen. 1:5

He DIVIDES – Gen. 1:7

He BLESSES – Gen. 1:28

364. SEVEN THINGS IN 1 COR. 2

Things UNKNOWN – 1 Cor. 2:9

Things PREPARED – 1 Cor. 2:9

Things REVEALED – 1 Cor. 2:10

Things DEEP – 1 Cor. 2:10

Things SEARCHED – 1 Cor. 2:10

Things FREE – 1 Cor. 2:12

Things WE SPEAK – 1 Cor. 2:13

365. SEVEN THINGS IN PSALM 61

DISTANCE – Psa. 61:2

DISTRESS – Psa. 61:2

DELIVERANCE – Psa. 61:2

DEFENSE – Psa. 61:3

DWELLING – Psa. 61:4

DESTINY – Psa. 61:7

DETERMINATION – Psa. 61:8

366. SEVEN THINGS OPENED

HEAVEN – Acts 7:56

The GRAVES – Matt. 27:52

The SCRIPTURES – Luke 24:32

The UNDERSTANDING – Luke 24:45

The DOOR – 1 Cor. 16:9

The HEART – Acts 16:14

The BOOKS – Rev. 20:12

367. SEVEN THINGS THE BLIND MAN DID

He HEARD – Luke 18:36

He CRIED – Luke 18:38

He CAME – Luke 18:40

He SPOKE – Luke 18:41

He RECEIVED – Luke 18:42

He FOLLOWED – Luke 18:43

He GLORIFIED – Luke 18:43

368. SEVEN THINGS THE FATHER DID

He SAW him – Luke 15:20

He had COMPASSION on him – Luke 15:20

He KISSED him – Luke 15:20

He CLOTHED him – Luke 15:22

He put SHOES on his feet – Luke 15:22

He FED him – Luke 15:23

He REJOICED over him – Luke 15:24

369. SEVENFOLD PRIVILEGE IN – MATT. 6

GIVING – Matt. 6:3, 4

PRAYING – Matt. 6:6

FORGIVING – Matt. 6:14

FASTING – Matt. 6:16-18

INSURING – Matt. 6:20

CONSIDERING – Matt. 6:28

SEEKING – Matt. 6:33

370. SEVENFOLD PRIVILEGE OF THE CHILD OF GOD
SAVED – Deu. 33:29

SECURED – Deu. 33:3

SEPARATED – Deu. 33:16

SATISFIED – Deu. 33:23

SHELTERED – Deu. 33:29

SEATED – Deu. 33:3

SACRIFICING – Deu. 33:19

371. A SEVENFOLD RESPONSIBILITY
Love all men – 1 Thess. 3:12

Be patient with all men – 1 Thess. 5:14

Live peaceably with all men – Rom. 12:18

Provide things honest in the sight of all – Rom. 12:17

Be gentle to all men – 2 Tim. 2:24

Let your moderation be known to all – Phil. 4:5

Let us do good unto all men – Gal. 6:10

372. A SEVENFOLD RESPONSIBILITY IN JUDE
CONTENDING – v.3

REMEMBERING – v.17

BUILDING – v.20

PRAYING – v.20

KEEPING – v.21

LOOKING – v.21

PRESENTING – v.24

373. A SEVENFOLD TESTIMONY
Show forth His DEATH – 1 Cor. 11:26

Show PIETY – 1 Tim. 5:4

Show Proof of your LOVE – 2 Cor. 8:24

Show FAITH – James 2:18

Show PRAISES – Isa. 60:6

Show MEEKNESS – Tit. 3:2

Show DILIGENCE – Heb. 6:11

374. A SEVENFOLD VIEW OF THE LOVE OF GOD
It is INFINITE — in its character – John 17:23

It is CONSTRAINING — in its power – 2 Cor. 5:14

It is INSEPARABLE — in its object – Rom. 8:35-37

It is INDIVIDUAL — in its choice – Gal. 2:20

It is UNIVERSAL — in its extent – John 3:16

It is UNCHANGING — in its purpose – John 13:1

It is EVERLASTING — in its duration – Jer. 31:3

375. THE SHEPHERD
A GOOD Shepherd – John 10:11

A GREAT Shepherd – Heb. 13:20

An EXPERIENCED Shepherd – Eze. 33:11

A GENTLE Shepherd – Isa. 40:11

A PATIENT Shepherd – Luke 15:4

A PERSONAL Shepherd – Psa. 23:1

The CHIEF Shepherd – 1 Pet. 5:4

376. SIN

The SERVANTS – Rom. 6:20

The WAGES – Rom. 6:23

The DECEITFULNESS – Heb. 3:13

The PLEASURES – Heb. 11:25

The SACRIFICE – Heb. 10:12

The ETERNAL CONSEQUENCES – Jude v.7

377. SIX ASPECTS OF LIFE

The SOURCE of life – 1 John 5:11

The SECURITY of life – Col. 3:3

The GIFT of life – Rom. 6:23

The CHARACTER of life – John 10:28

The ABUNDANCE of life – John 10:10

The CROWN of life – James 1:12

378. SIX GOOD THINGS IN 1 TIMOTHY

The good LAW – 1 Tim. 1:8

The good WARFARE – 1 Tim. 1:18

The good CONSCIENCE – 1 Tim. 1:19

The good SERVICE – 1 Tim. 5:4

The good FIGHT – 1 Tim. 6:12

The good WORKS – 1 Tim. 5:25

379. SIX POINTS IN PHILIPPIANS 3

CAUTIONING – v.2

COUNTING – v.8

CONFORMING – v.10

CALLING – v.14

CONVERSING – v.20

CHANGING – v.21

380. SOME NEGLECTED EXHORTATIONS
Know them that are over you – 1 Thess. 5:12 – How ? By the services they render to the saints.

Remember them which have the rule over you – Heb. 13:7 – Why? As an example worthy to follow.

Obey them that have the rule over you – Heb. 13:17 – How? By submitting yourselves, because they feel their responsibility for your soul's welfare and growth in grace.

Salute them that have the rule over you – Heb. 13:24

381. THE SONS OF ELI
Their CHARACTER – 1 Sam. 2:12

Their IGNORANCE – 1 Sam. 2:12

Their SIN – 1 Sam. 2:17

Their PRIVILEGE – 1 Sam. 2:25

Their WARNING – 1 Sam. 2:34

Their DOOM – 1 Sam. 4:11

382. THE SOUL
The soul REDEEMED – Psa. 49:8

The soul DELIVERED – Psa. 33:19

The soul PRECIOUS – 1 Sam. 26:21

The soul LONGING – Psa. 107:9

The soul GENEROUS – Prov. 11:25

The soul DELIGHTING – Isa. 55:2

The soul FRUITFUL – Jer. 31:12

383. SPIRITUAL BLESSINGS
"Blessed with all spiritual blessings in Christ" from Ephesians chapter 1

An election that cannot be annulled

A relationship that cannot be broken

An acceptance that cannot be questioned

A title that cannot be disputed

A forgiveness that cannot be modified

A union that cannot be dissolved

An inheritance that cannot fade away

A seal that cannot be disowned

A pledge that cannot be dishonored

from Ephesians Chapter 2

A life that cannot be forfeited

A peace that cannot be destroyed

A foundation that cannot be removed

384. STAGES OF CHRISTIANITY
A Christian by Calling – Acts 11:26

A Christian by Persuasion – Acts 26:29

A Christian by Suffering – 1 Pet. 4:16

385. STRONG IN THE LORD
Strength in TEMPTATION – 2 Cor. 12:7-9

Strength in TROUBLE – Psa. 37:39

Strength in SICKNESS – Psa. 41:3

Strength in WEAKNESS – Isa. 40:29

Strength in SERVICE Hag 2:4

Strength in WARFARE – 2 Sam. 22:40

Strength in WAITING – Isa. 30:7

386. SUBJECTS OF DISCOURSE IN JOHN 4
The WATER – vv.7-15

The HUSBAND – vv.16-18

The WORSHIP – vv.19-24

The MESSIAH – vv.25-26

387. SUBJECTS OF PAUL'S ADDRESS AT ATHENS
REPENTANCE – Acts 17:30

RIGHTEOUSNESS – Acts 17:31

RESURRECTION – Acts 17:31

RETRIBUTION – Acts 17:31

388. A SUM IN MULTIPLICATION
PARDON Multiplied – Isa. 55:7

GRACE Multiplied – 2 Pet. 1:2

PEACE Multiplied – 2 Pet. 1:2

LOVE Multiplied – Jude v.2

With MEEKNESS Multiplied – Psa. 18:35

PROVISION Multiplied – Matt. 14:15-20

SEED Multiplied – 2 Cor. 9:10

WORD Multiplied – Acts 12:24

DISCIPLES Multiplied – Acts 6:1

389. TEARS
The SAVIOR'S tears – John 11:35

The SINNER'S tears – Luke 7:38

The BACKSLIDER'S tears – Luke 22:62

ESAU'S tears – Heb. 12:17

APOSTLE'S tears – Acts 20:19

390. THE TEN LEPERS
CONDITION they were in – Luke 17:12

POSITION they occupied – Luke 17:12

PRAYER they offered – Luke 17:13

FAITH they exercised – Luke 17:14

THANKSGIVING they rendered – Luke 17:15, 16

391. TEN STEPS IN ISRAEL'S EXPERIENCE IN THE WILDERNESS
Their SIN — "Spoke against God" – Num. 21:5

Their CONFESSION — "We have sinned" – Num. 21:7

Their SALVATION — "He lived" – Num. 21:8

Their PILGRIMAGE — "They journeyed " – Num. 21:11

Their REFRESHMENT — "I will give them water" – Num. 21:16

Their SINGING — "Then Israel sang" – Num. 21:17

Their COMMUNION — "Top of Pisgah" – Num. 21:20

Their CONFLICT — "Sihon fought with Israel" – Num. 21:23

Their VICTORY — "Israel smote him" – Num. 21:24

Their ENCOURAGEMENT — "Fear him not." – Num. 21:34

392. TEN STEPS IN THE PRODIGAL'S LIFE
His DEMAND — "Give...portion" – Luke 15:12

His DEPARTURE — "Took...Journey" – Luke 15:13

His DISTRESS — "Famine" – Luke 15:14

His CONDITION — "In want" – Luke 15:14

His DEPRAVITY — "Feeding Swine" – Luke 15:15

His CONVICTION — "Came to himself" – Luke 15:17

His DETERMINATION — "I will arise" – Luke 15:18

His CONFESSION — "I have sinned" – Luke 15:18

His CONTRITION — "No more worthy" – Luke 15:19

His CONVERSION — "The best robe, &c." – Luke 15:22

393. THERE SHALL BE SHOWERS OF BLESSING
The CERTAINTY of it — "Shall." – Eze. 34:26

The ABUNDANCE of it — "Showers." – Eze. 34:26

The CHARACTER of it — "Blessing." – Eze. 34:26

394. THINGS RESERVED
Inheritance – 1 Pet. 1:4

Angels who sinned – 2 Pet. 2:4

Unjust – 2 Pet. 2:9

Darkness – 2 Pet. 2:17

Heaven and earth – 2 Pet. 3:7

Wrath – Nah. 1:2

395. THINGS THAT ARE OPENED
The WINDOW for blessing – Mal. 3:10

The BOOK for instruction – Neh. 8:5

The EAR for listening – Isa. 50:5

The MOUTH for testimony – Eph. 6:19

The DOOR for admission – Acts 14:27

The HEART for reception – Acts 16:14

The EYES for seeing – Acts 9:8

396. THINGS TO BE FULL OF
Full of the SPIRIT – Eph. 5:18

Full of LIGHT – Matt. 6:22

Full of JOY – John 15:11

Full of GOOD WORKS – Acts 9:36

Full of POWER – Micah 3:8

Full of GLORY – 1 Pet. 1:8

397. THINGS WEIGHED BY GOD
ACTIONS – 1 Sam. 2:3

WATERS – Job 28:25

SPIRITS – Prov. 16:2

MOUNTAINS – Isa. 40:12

PATH of the just – Isa. 26:7

MAN – Dan. 5:27

398. THINGS WELL PLEASING TO GOD
Six things with which the Lord is well pleased.

With His beloved Son – Matt. 3:17

His righteousness sake – Isa. 42:21

With many sacrifices of doing good and sharing – Heb. 13:16

The working out in us of all the will of God – Heb. 13:21

The obedience of children to parents – Col. 3:20

The gifts of saints to servants – Phil. 4:18

399. THOSE DELIVERED FROM CAPTIVITY WERE —
SEATED – Neh. 10:1

SEPARATED – Neh. 10:28

INSTRUCTED – Neh. 10:28

UNITED – Neh. 10:29

FAITHFUL – Neh. 10:29

DEVOTED – Neh. 10:32

400. THOUGHTS FROM JOHN 17
The Father spoken of in a threefold way —

"O Father" — in connection with His Son – v.5

"Holy Father" — in connection with believers – v.11

"Righteous Father" — in connection with the world – v.25

401. THREE ABOMINATIONS
SACRIFICE of the Wicked – Prov. 15:8

WAY of the Wicked – Prov. 15:9

THOUGHTS of the Wicked – Prov. 15:26

402. THREE ASPECTS OF GRACE
Grace ANNOUNCED – Tit. 1:4

Grace APPEARING – Tit. 2:11

Grace JUSTIFYING – Tit. 3:7

403. THREE ASPECTS OF JUDGMENT
The INDIVIDUALITY of it – Rev. 20:13

The RIGHTEOUSNESS of it – Rom. 2:5

The DURATION of it – Heb. 6:2

404. THREE ASPECTS OF KNOWLEDGE
Knowledge of His GRACE – Col. 1:6

Knowledge of His WILL – Col. 1:9

Knowledge of HIMSELF – Col. 1:10

405. THREE ASPECTS OF PEACE
Peace WITHIN – Luke 24:36

Peace BELOW – Luke 2:14

Peace ABOVE – Luke 19:38

406. THREE ASPECTS OF WORK
Work of the GOSPEL – 1 Thess. 1:3

Work of my HANDS – 1 Thess. 4:11

Work in the CHURCH – 1 Thess. 5:13

407. THREE ATTITUDES OF THE BELIEVER
SITTING – Eph. 2:6

STANDING – Eph. 6:14

WALKING – Eph. 5:2, 8

408. THREE BUNDLES
Bundle of LIFE – 1 Sam. 25:29

Bundle of MYRRH – Song 1:13

Bundle of TARES – Matt. 13:30

409. THREE CLASSES IN NUMBERS
The WARRIORS – Num. 1

The WORKERS – Num. 2

The WORSHIPPERS – Num. 3

410. THREE COMMANDS
Put OFF – Eph. 4:22

Put ON – Eph. 4:24

Put AWAY – Eph. 4:25

411. THREE CONCLUSIONS
Concluded all under SIN – Gal. 3:22

Concluded all in UNBELIEF – Rom. 11:32

Concluded — A man is justified by faith – Rom. 3:28

412. THREE CRIES
Cry of one who was in DANGER – Matt. 14:30

Cry of one who was in NEED – Mark 10:47

Cry of one who was LOST – Luke 16:24

413. THREE CRIES FROM THREE CLASSES
The Christian — "Come, Lord Jesus!" – Rev. 22:20

Unjust Servant — "My Master is delayed." – Matt. 24:48

The Scoffer — "Where is the promise?" – 2 Pet. 3:4

414. THREE CUPS IN LUKE 22
Cup of the PASSOVER – Luke 22:17

Cup of BLESSING – Luke 22:20

Cup of SORROW – Luke 22:42

415. THREE ENQUIRERS
The ANXIOUS – Acts 16:30

The CURIOUS – Luke 13:23

The SCOFFING – Isa. 21:11

416. THREE EXCUSES
The first man had something to see – Luke 14:18

The second man had something to prove – Luke 14:19

The third man had someone to love – Luke 14:20

417. THREE FORMS OF CORRUPTION
CORRUPTION BY SACRIFICE – The doctrine of Balaam – Rev. 2:14

CORRUPTION BY AUTHORITY – The doctrine of the Nicolaitans – Rev. 2:15

CORRUPTION BY INFLUENCE – The doctrine of Jezebel – Rev. 2:20

418. THREE GIFTS FROM THE FATHER TO THE SON
POWER – John 17:2

PEOPLE – John 17:6

GLORY – John 17:24

419. THREE GIFTS FROM THE LORD TO US
Life that can never be forfeited – John 17:2

Word that will never pass away – John 17:14

Glory that will ever be manifested – John 17:22

420. THREE GREAT EVENTS
HE came – Matt. 25:10

THEY went in – Matt. 25:10

The DOOR was shut – Matt. 25:10

421. THREE GREAT REALITIES IN HEBREWS
The great SALVATION – Heb. 2:3

The great HIGH PRIEST – Heb. 4:14

The great SHEPHERD of the Sheep – Heb. 13:20

422. THREE HARVESTS
PAST – Jer. 8:20

PRESENT – Matt. 9:37

FUTURE – Matt. 13:39

423. THREE IMPOSSIBILITIES IN HEBREWS
IMPOSSIBLE to renew them again – Heb. 6:4

IMPOSSIBLE for God to lie – Heb. 6:18

IMPOSSIBLE to please God without faith – Heb. 11:6

424. THREE "MUSTS" OF JOHN 3
The Sinner's must – "You MUST be born again" – verse 7

The Savior's must – "So MUST the Son of Man be lifted up" – verse 15

The Sovereign's must – "He MUST increase" – verse 30

425. THREE PLACES WHERE GOD PUT THE NAMES OF THE TRIBES
On the SHOULDERS — the place of strength – Exo. 28:12

On the HEART — the place of affection – Exo. 28:29

On the FOREHEAD — the place of thought — Exo. 28:38

426. THREE QUESTIONS IN JEREMIAH
What have I done? – Jer. 8:6

What will you do? – Jer. 12:5

What will you say? – Jer. 13:21

427. THREE REIGNS
DEATH reigning – Rom. 5:17

LIFE reigning – Rom. 5:17

GRACE reigning – Rom. 5:21

428. THREE REPRESENTATIVE MEN
MOSES the man of God – 1 Chron. 23:14

SOLOMON the man of rest – 1 Chron. 22:9

DAVID the man of war – 1 Sam. 16:18

429. THREE SCENES
Scene on EARTH – Luke 14:23

Scene in HEAVEN – Luke 15:7

Scene in HELL – Luke 16:23

430. THREE STAGES In DISCIPLINE
Purge out – 1 Cor. 5:7

Come out – 2 Cor. 6:17

Spew out – Rev. 3:16

431. THREE THINGS IN GENESIS 15:1
ENCOURAGEMENT – "Fear not."

SECURITY – "Your shield."

RECOMPENSE – "Great reward."

432. THREE THINGS IN HABAKKUK
The EAR OPENED – Hab. 2:1

The MESSAGE HEARD – Hab. 2:2

The EFFECTS PRODUCED – Hab. 3:16

433. THREE THINGS MUST BE CLEAN
Clean HEART for worship – Psa. 51:10, 17

Clean HANDS for work – Psa. 24:4

Clean FEET for walk – John 13:5

434. THREE THINGS OPENED
The HEART opened — (salvation) – Acts 16:14

The PRISON opened — (liberty) – Acts 16:26

The HOUSE opened — (fellowship) – Acts 16:15

435. THREE THINGS PROMISED TO JACOB
Divine COMPANIONSHIP "I am with you."

Divine GUARDIANSHIP "And will keep."

Divine GUIDANCE "And will bring."

436. THREE TRUMPETS
Trumpet of GRACE – Lev. 25:9

Trumpet of GLORY – 1 Cor. 15:52

Trumpet of JUDGMENT – Josh. 6:4-5

437. THREEFOLD INVITATION
Come unto Me – Matt. 11:28

Come after Me – Matt. 16:24

Come follow Me – Matt. 4:19

438. THREEFOLD KEEPING
The FATHER Keeping us – John 17:11

The SON Keeping us – John 17:12

US Keeping His Word – John 17:6

439. THREEFOLD LOVE
God the Father – John 3:16

Jesus the Son – Eph. 5:25

The Holy Spirit – Rom. 15:30

440. THREEFOLD OBJECT OF THE LORD'S COMING
Coming to RECEIVE – Matt. 25:6

Coming to RECKON – Matt. 25:19

Coming to JUDGE – Matt. 25:31

441. THREEFOLD REST
Rest GIVEN – Matt. 11:28

Rest FOUND – Matt. 11:29

Rest REMAINING – Heb. 4:9

442. "TILL HE COME"
WORKING – Luke 19:13

FOLLOWING – John 21:22, 23

REMEMBERING – 1 Cor. 11:23, 26

HOLDING FAST – Rev. 2:25

443. 2 TIMOTHY 3
We have PREDICTION – v.1

We have ILLUSTRATION – vv.8-9

We have EXHORTATION – v.14

444. TITLES OF CHRIST IN JOHN 1
The WORD – v.1

The LIFE – v.4

The LIGHT – v.7

The ONLY BEGOTTEN OF THE FATHER – v.14

JESUS CHRIST – v.17

The LORD – v.23

The LAMB – v.29

The SON OF GOD – v.34

MASTER – v.38

JESUS OF NAZARETH – v.45

SON OF JOSEPH – v.45

KING OF ISRAEL – v.49

SON OF MAN – v.51

445. TO HIMSELF
Reconciled to Himself – Col. 1:20

Subdued to Himself – Phil. 3:21

Purified to Himself – Titus 2:14

Presented to Himself – Eph. 5:27

446. TOGETHER
GATHERING together – Ezra 3:1

STANDING together – Ezra 3:9

SINGING together – Ezra 3:11

BUILDING together – Ezra 4:3

COMFORTING   5:11

LIVING together – 1 Thess. 5:10

CAUGHT UP together – 1 Thess. 4:17

447. THE TREE
Adam BEHIND the tree – Gen. 3:8

Nathanael UNDER the tree – John 1:48

Zacchaeus up IN the tree – Luke 19:4

Jesus ON the tree – Acts 5:30

448. THE TRINITY
The FATHER, spoken of as the Bosom – John 1:18

The SON, spoken of as the Lamb – John 1:29

The HOLY SPIRIT, spoken of as the Dove – John 1:32

449. TRUST IN THE LORD
Trust in the Lord at all times – Psa. 62:8

Trust Him for strength – Isa. 26:4

Trust Him for guidance – Psa. 37:5

Trust Him in the dark – Isa. 50:10

Trust Him with all your heart – Pro. 3:5

Trust Him through he slay you – Job 13.15

450. TRUTHS CONNECTED WITH THE HOLY SPIRIT
THE HOLY SPIRIT

Convicts the world – John 16:8-12

Regenerates the believing one – John 3:5-7; 1 John 5:7

Indwells the child of God – John 14:17

Seals the saint – Eph. 1:13

Is the comforter and guide – John 15:26; 16:13

Is the unction or holy anointing – 1 John 2:20

Is the earnest of coming glory – Eph. 1:14

THE CHRISTIAN IS EXHORTED TO

Be filled with the Spirit – Eph. 5:18

Pray in the Spirit – Jude v.20; Eph. 6:18

Sing in the Spirit – Eph. 5:19

Worship in the Spirit – John 4:23; Phil. 3:3

Walk in the Spirit – Gal. 5:16

Be led by the Spirit – Gal. 5:18

Remember His Body is the temple of the Holy Spirit – 1 Cor. 6:19

451. TWO DESIRES
The JEWS wishing to see Lazarus – John 12:9

The GREEKS wishing to see Jesus – John 12:21

452. TWO MARVELS
He marveled at the FAITH of a Gentile – Matt. 8:10

He marveled at the UNBELIEF of the Jews – Mark 6:6

453. TWO POSTAL DELIVERIES
I. Message of DEATH – Est. 3:13

    1. It was universal — "all" – Est. 3:13

    2. It brought

        Trouble – Est. 3:15

        Bitterness – Est. 4:1

        Humility – Est. 4:3

        Weeping – Est. 4:3

II. Message of Life – Est. 8:11

    1. It was universal – Est. 8:11

    2. It brought

        Light – Est. 8:16

        Gladness – Est. 8:16

        Joy – Est. 8:16

        Feasting – Est. 8:17

        A good day – Est. 8:17

454. TWO PRAYERS IN MARK 5
The GADARENES Prayed Christ to Depart – Mark 5:17

The MAN HEALED Prayed to be with Christ – Mark 5:18

455. TWO THINGS — UNQUENCHABLE
The LOVE which shows forth His grace – Song 8:7

The FIRE which shows forth His judgment – Luke 3:17

456. TWOFOLD CHARGE AGAINST ISRAEL
They have FORSAKEN Me – Jer. 2:13

They have FORGOTTEN Me – Jer. 2:32

457. TWOFOLD SATISFACTION
Christ's – Isa. 53:11

Believer's – Psa. 17:15

458. UNITED IN
In PRAYER – Acts 2:1

In WORK – Ezra 3:9

In WORSHIP – Ezra 3:1-4

In PRAISE – 2 Chron. 5:13

459. UNITY
One mind in the Gospel – Phil. 1:27

One mind in the likeness to Jesus – Phil. 2:5

One mind as to Progress– Phil. 3:12-15

One mind as to our Walk – Phil. 4:2

460. UNIVERSAL DEPRAVITY
All out of the way – Rom. 3:12

All have sinned – Rom. 3:23

All are guilty – Rom. 3:19

All are in unbelief – Rom. 11:32

461. UNSEARCHABLE RICHES
Rich in MERCY – Eph. 2:4

Rich in GRACE – Eph. 1:7

Rich in INHERITANCE – Eph. 1:18

Rich in GLORY – Eph. 3:16

462. THE VALLEY

A place of BLESSING – 2 Chron. 20:26

A place of DECISION – Joel 3:14

A place of HOPE – Hos. 2:15

A place of FRUITFULNESS – Num. 32:9

A place of CONFIDENCE – – Psa. 23:4

A place of REFRESHMENT – – Psa. 84:6

A place of VICTORY – 1 Sam. 17:2, 51

463. WAITING

I. For WHOM we wait

    The Lord – – Psa. 37:7

    The Son – 1 Thess. 1:10

II. How LONG we wait – – Psa. 25:5

III. HOW to wait – – Psa. 37:7

IV. For WHAT we wait

    The Salvation – Gen. 49:18; – Rom. 13:11

    The Hope – Gal. 5:5

    Our Manifestation – Rom. 8:19

V. RESULT of waiting

    Renewing – Isa. 40:31

    Mounting – Isa. 40:31

    Running — not weary – Isa. 40:31

Walking — not faint – Isa. 40:31

Happiness – Isa. 30:18

Goodness – Lam. 3:25

464. THE WATER OF LIFE
I. Its Character

Living – John 4:10

Clear – Rev. 22:1

Pure – Rev. 22:1

Abundant – Eze. 47:1-9

Free – Rev. 21:6

II. For whom provided.

The Thirsty – Rev. 21:6

Whosoever – Rev. 22:17

III. Way to obtain it.

Come – Rev. 22:17

Take – Rev. 22:17

465. WATER IN MOTION
The water put in – John 3:5

The water springing up – John 4:14

The water flowing out – John 7:38

466. WE ARE TO BE
Sound in MIND – 2 Tim. 1:7

Sound in DOCTRINE – Tit. 1:9

Sound in FAITH – Tit. 1:13

Sound in SPEECH — Tit. 2:8

467. WE SEE JESUS
Crowned with glory and honor — Heb. 2:9

The Author and Finisher of our faith — Heb. 12:2

A Guarantor — Heb. 7:22

A High Priest forever — Heb. 6:20

> A High Priest, holy, harmless. undefiled, separate from sinners — Heb. 7:26
>
> A merciful High Priest — Heb. 2:17
>
> A great High Priest — Heb. 4:14
>
> A High Priest who is set on the right hand of the Majesty in the heavens — Heb. 8:1

468. WEAK THINGS
An ox goad — Judges 3:21

A woman — Judges 4:4

A nail — Judges 4:21

Pitchers and trumpets — Judges 7:20

A piece of millstone — Judges 9:53

Jaw bone of an ass — Judges 15:16

469. WHAT A CHILD OF GOD SHOULD HAVE
Christ in his heart — Col. 1:27

Glory in his face — Acts 6:15

The Spirit as his teacher — John 14:26

Fear of God to guide him — Pro. 8:13

Path of holiness to walk in — Isa. 35:8

Heaven as his destination – John 14:2

470. WHAT CHRIST DECLARES HIMSELF TO BE
I am the LIGHT of the world – John 8:12

I am the WAY – John 14:6

I am the GOOD SHEPHERD – John 10:11

I am the DOOR of the sheep – John 10:7

I am the BREAD of LIFE – John 6:35

I am the TRUE VINE – John 15:1

I am the RESURRECTION and the LIFE – John 11:25

471. WHAT CHRIST HAS DONE FOR US
Died for us – 1 Cor. 15:3

Made us alive – Eph. 2:5

Begotten us – 1 Pet. 1:4

Bore our sins – 1 Pet. 2:24

Translated us – Col. 1:13

Raised us – Eph. 2:6

Loved us – Rev. 1:5

Made us kings – Rev. 1:6

Given us the victory – 1 Cor. 15:57

Saved us – Titus 3:5

Called us – 2 Tim. 1:9

Washed us – Rev. 1:5

Delivered us – 2 Cor. 1:10

Blessed us – Eph. 1:3

472. WHAT DANIEL WAS
A SEPARATED man – Dan. 1:8

A CONSISTENT man – Dan. 6:2

A FAITHFUL man – Dan. 6:4

A BOLD man – Dan. 6:10

A PRAYERFUL man – Dan. 6:10

A THANKFUL man – Dan. 6:10

A DILIGENT man – Dan. 6:16

A PROSPEROUS man – Dan. 6:28

473. WHAT KIND OF MAN WAS DAVID?
From 1 Samuel 18

An accepted man – v.5

A persecuted man – v.11

A wise man – v.14

A loved man – v.16

A humble man – v.18

A valiant man – v.27

A precious man – v.30

474. WHAT IS NIGH?
The LORD – Psa. 34:18

His PEOPLE – Eph. 2:13

The COMING – James 5:8

The DELIVERANCE – Luke 21:28

The WORD – Rom. 10:8

The JUDGMENT Joe 2:1

475. WHAT JESUS DID FOR US
Made us WHOLE – Matt. 9:22

Made PEACE for us – Col. 1:20

Made us ACCEPTED – Eph. 1:6

Made us FREE – Rom. 8:2

Made us to REST – Eph. 2:6

Made us to PROSPER – 2 Chron. 26:5

Made us KINGS – Rev. 1:6

476. WHAT JONATHAN DID TO DAVID
LOVED Him – 1 Sam. 18:1

CLOTHED Him – 1 Sam. 18:4

GAVE ALL to Him – 1 Sam. 18:4

SAVED Him – 1 Sam. 19:2

STRENGTHENED Him – 1 Sam. 23:16

DELIGHTED in Him – 1 Sam. 19:2

ENCOURAGED Him – 1 Sam. 23:17

477. WHAT THE LORD DOES FOR US IN PSALM 34
He REDEEMS us – v.22

He SAVES us – v.18

He HEARS us – v.4

He DELIVERS us – v.4

He PRESERVES us – v.7

He is INTERESTED in us – v.15

He is NEAR us – v.18

478. WHAT TO INCREASE IN: —
FAITH – Luke 17:5

LOVE – 1 Thess. 3:12

JOY – Isa. 29:19

GREATNESS – Psa. 71:21

STRENGTH – Isa. 40:29

KNOWLEDGE – Col. 1:10

BLESSING – 1 Cor. 3:6, 7

479. WHAT WE ARE
SONS – Rom. 8:14

SAINTS – Rom. 1:7

KINGS – Rev. 1:6

PRIESTS – Rev. 1:6

BRANCHES – John 15:5

COMPLETE – Col. 2:10

LIGHTS – Phil. 2:15

SALT – Matt. 5:13

EPISTLES – 2 Cor. 3:2

480. WHAT WE ARE ABLE TO DO
Able to STAND – Eph. 6:11

Able to WITHSTAND – Eph. 6:13

Able to QUENCH – Eph. 6:16

Able to INSTRUCT – 2 Tim. 2:2

Able to ADMONISH – Rom. 15:14

Able to EXHORT – Tit. 1:9

Able to GIVE – Ezra 2:69

Able to OVERCOME – Num. 13:30

481. WHAT WE ARE NOT TO DO
FRET not – Psa. 37:7-8

FORSAKE not My law – Prov. 4:2

FORGET not to do good – Heb. 13:16

FAINT not; we shall reap – Gal. 6:9

FEAR not...you are Mine – Isa. 43:1

FORBID him not – Luke 9:50

482. WHAT WE DO BY FAITH
We LIVE by faith – Gal. 2:20

We STAND by faith – 2 Cor. 1:24

We WALK by faith – 2 Cor. 5:7

We ENDURE by faith – Heb. 11:27

We SUBDUE by faith – Heb. 11:33

We FIGHT by faith – 1 Tim. 6:12

We OVERCOME by faith – 1 John 5:4

483. WHAT WE HAVE
LIFE – 1 John 5:11

PEACE – Rom. 5:1

ACCESS – Eph. 2:18

ASSURANCE – Col. 2:2

GUIDANCE – Psa. 32:8

FELLOWSHIP – 1 John 1:3

SUFFICIENCY – 2 Cor. 9:8

ADVOCACY – 1 John 2:1

484. WHAT WE OUGHT TO BE

REJOICING – Phil. 3:1

CONTENDING – Jude v.3

WATCHING – Luke 12:37

PRAYING – Eph. 6:18

GIVING – Rom. 12:8

RUNNING – Heb. 12:1

OVERCOMING – Rev. 3:21

WAITING – 1 Thess. 1:10

485. WHAT WE OUGHT TO DO

We ought always to pray – Luke 18:1

We ought to wash one another's feet – John 13:14

We ought to obey God – Acts 5:29

We ought to bear the infirmities of the weak – Rom. 15:1

We ought to give earnest heed – Heb. 2:1

We ought to walk as He walked – 1 John 2:6

We ought to lay down our lives – 1 John 3:16

We ought also to love one another – 1 John 4:11

We ought to receive His witnesses – 3 John 1:8

486. WHAT WE RECEIVE

CHRIST – Col. 2:6

FORGIVENESS – Acts 10:43

MERCY – 2 Cor. 4:1

GRACE – Rom. 1:5

HOLY SPIRIT – Acts 10:47

End of FAITH (Salvation) – 1 Pet. 1:9

KINGDOM – Heb. 12:28

COMMANDMENT – 2 John 1:4

CROWN – James 1:12

487. WHAT WE SHALL BE

RAISED – 1 Cor. 15:52

CHANGED – 1 Cor. 15:52

MANIFESTED – 2 Cor. 5:10

SPOTLESS – Eph. 5:27

PRESENTED – Eph. 5:27

We shall APPEAR WITH Him – Col. 3:4

488. WILDERNESS PROVISION in Psalm 23

THE LORD IS MY SHEPHERD, I SHALL NOT WANT

1. I shall not want rest.

    Verse 2 — He maketh me to lie down in green pastures.

2. I shall not want refreshment.

    Verse 2—He leadeth me beside the still waters.

3. I shall not want restoration.

Verse 3—He restoreth my soul.

4. I shall not want counsel.

    Verse 3—He leadeth me in the paths of righteousness.

5. I shall not want companionship.

    Verse 4— For Thou art with me.

6. I shall not want comfort.

    Verse 4—Thy rod and Thy staff, they comfort me.

7. I shall not want provender.

    Verse 5—Thou preparest a table before me.

8. I shall not want power.

    Verse 5 – Thou anointest my head with oil.

9. I shall not want anything here.

    Verse 6 – Goodness and mercy shall follow me all the days of my life.

10. I shall not want anything here after.

Verse 6 – I will dwell in the House of the Lord forever.

489. WOMAN IN SIMON'S HOUSE

Her CONDITION — "A sinner" – Luke 7:37

Her POSITION — "At His feet" – Luke 7:38

Her CONTRITION — "Weeping" – Luke 7:38

Her FAITH — "Your faith" – Luke 7:50

Her FORGIVENESS — "Your sins are forgiven" – Luke 7:48

Her SALVATION — "Saved you" – Luke 7:50

Her PLACE — "Go in peace" – Luke 7:50

490. THE WOMAN WITH THE ISSUE OF BLOOD

She HEARD – Mark 5:27

She CAME – Mark 5:27

She TOUCHED – Mark 5:27

She TRUSTED – Mark 5:28

She WAS HEALED – Mark 5:29

She KNEW – Mark 5:29

She CONFESSED – Mark 5:33

491. THE WORD OF GOD

What it is —

    The SON OF GOD – John 1:14

    Likened to SEED – Luke 8:11

    Likened to a SWORD – Eph. 6:17

    Likened to a FIRE – Jer. 23:29

    Likened to a HAMMER – Jer. 23:29

The character of it —

    POWERFUL – Heb. 4:12

    PURE – Prov. 30:5

    UNALTERABLE – Isa. 40:8

What we are to do with it —

    DESIRE it – 1 Pet. 2:2

    RECEIVE it – James 1:21

    KEEP it – John 17:6

    HOLD it fast – Tit. 1:9

PREACH It – 2 Tim. 4:2

REMEMBER it – Luke 24:8

Be DOERS of it – James 1:22

The effect of the Word —

We are QUICKENED by it – Psa. 119:25

We are BORN AGAIN by it – 1 Pet. 1:23

We are CLEANSED by it – Psa. 119:9

We are SANCTIFIED by it – John 17:17

We are STRENGTHENED by it – Psa. 119:28

We OVERCOME by it – Rev. 12:11

492. WORDS OF EXHORTATION

Let us fear lest, a promise being left of entering into His rest, any of you should seem to come short of it – Hebrews 4:1

Let us labor to enter into that rest – Heb. 4:11

Let us hold fast – Heb. 4:14 ; 10:23

Let us come boldly to the throne of grace – Heb. 4:16

Let us draw near with a true heart – Heb. 10:22

Let us go on unto perfection – Heb. 6:1

Let us lay aside every weight – Heb. 12:1

Let us run with patience . . . looking unto Jesus – Heb. 12:1-2

Let us go forth unto Him without the camp – Heb. 13:13

Let us offer the sacrifice of praise . . . continually – Heb. 13:15

Let us have grace whereby we may serve God acceptably – Heb. 12:28

493. THE WORK OF CHRIST FOR ME
Jesus DIED to redeem me – Eph. 1:7

Jesus was RAISED to justify me – Rom. 4:25

Jesus lives to INTERCEDE for me – Heb. 7:25

Jesus is coming again to SATISFY me – Psa. 17:15

494. WORKING FOR GOD
EXHORTATION for the work — "Go" – Matt. 21:28

SPHERE for the work — "My Vineyard" – Matt. 21:28

SEASON for the work — "Today" – Matt. 21:28

POWER for the work — "Holy Spirit" – Acts 1:8

RESULT of the work — "Added," etc. – Acts 2:41

REWARD of the work — "Shall shine" – Dan. 12:3

495. WORTHY THINGS AND MEN
A Worthy Repentance – Luke 3:8

A Worthy Saying – 1 Tim. 1:15; 4:9

A Worthy Walk – Eph. 4:1; Col. 1:10; 1 Thess. 2:12

A Worthy Citizen – Luke 7:4

A Worthy Workman – Luke 10:7; 1 Tim. 6:1

A Worthy Escape – Luke 21:36

A Worthy Possessor – 2 Thess. 1:5

496. THE WRATH OF GOD
The duration of it – Rev. 14:10-11

The subjects of it – John 3:36

The certainty of it – 2 Thess. 2:11,12

The nature of it – 2 Thess. 1:9

The place of it – Rev. 21:8

497. YEAR OF JUBILEE
They had LIBERTY from bondage – Lev. 25:11

They had REST from toil – Lev. 25:11

They had ENTIRE SAFETY – Lev. 25:19

There was REDEMPTION of the land – Lev. 25:25

498. YOUR FAITH
Basis of Faith – Rom. 10:17

Object of Faith – Acts 27:25

Secret of Faith – Gal. 2:20

Trial of Faith – 1 Pet. 1:7

Power of Faith – Gal. 5:22

Prayer of Faith – James 5:15

Victory of Faith – 1 John 5:4

499. YOUR PATHS
Teach me Your paths – Psalm 25:4

Overflow with abundance – Psalm 65:11

Have held fast – Psalm 17:5

500. ZEALOUS
A Zealous Savior – John 2:17

A Zealous Spirit – Rom. 12:11

A Zealous Sinner – Phil. 3:6

A Zealous Service – Titus 2:14

A Zealous Saint – Acts 18:25

A Zealous Servant – Col. 4:12-13

A Zealous Shepherd – 2 Cor. 11:2

CONCLUSION

Thank you so much for investing in this ministry resource. We have many more sermon outlines and other resources available at: https://www.amazon.com/author/barrydavis and https://www.pastorshelper.com

My hope and prayer is that these resources help you in your mission to serve Christ and His Church. Our ministry is here to serve you and your needs in any way that we possibly can.

I hope to hear from you soon! May God bless you as you continue to serve Him.

In Christ,

Barry L. Davis

Made in the USA
Monee, IL
13 April 2023